Improving Financial Literacy

ANALYSIS OF ISSUES AND POLICIES

OECD

ORGANISATION FOR ECONOMIC CO-OPERATION AND DEVELOPMENT

ORGANISATION FOR ECONOMIC CO-OPERATION AND DEVELOPMENT

The OECD is a unique forum where the governments of 30 democracies work together to address the economic, social and environmental challenges of globalisation. The OECD is also at the forefront of efforts to understand and to help governments respond to new developments and concerns, such as corporate governance, the information economy and the challenges of an ageing population. The Organisation provides a setting where governments can compare policy experiences, seek answers to common problems, identify good practice and work to co-ordinate domestic and international policies.

The OECD member countries are: Australia, Austria, Belgium, Canada, the Czech Republic, Denmark, Finland, France, Germany, Greece, Hungary, Iceland, Ireland, Italy, Japan, Korea, Luxembourg, Mexico, the Netherlands, New Zealand, Norway, Poland, Portugal, the Slovak Republic, Spain, Sweden, Switzerland, Turkey, the United Kingdom and the United States. The Commission of the European Communities takes part in the work of the OECD.

OECD Publishing disseminates widely the results of the Organisation's statistics gathering and research on economic, social and environmental issues, as well as the conventions, guidelines and standards agreed by its members.

This work is published on the responsibility of the Secretary-General of the OECD. The opinions expressed and arguments employed herein do not necessarily reflect the official views of the Organisation or of the governments of its member countries.

Publié en français sous le titre :
Pour une meilleure éducation financière
ENJEUX ET INITIATIVES

Foreword

This book is the first major study of financial education at the international level. It highlights the economic, demographic and policy changes that make financial education increasingly important, identifies and analyses financial literacy surveys in OECD countries, describes the different types of financial education programmes currently being offered, evaluates their effectiveness to the extent possible, and suggests some actions policymakers can take to improve financial education and awareness.

The book begins with a definition of financial education that includes elements of information, instruction, and advice. Chapter 2 contains a brief discussion of the increasing importance of financial education as a result, in part, of the growing complexity and number of financial products, the approaching retirement of the baby boom and the increase in life expectancy, and changes in pension arrangements. It also describes the contributions of financial education to consumer well-being and market efficiency. An analysis of financial literacy surveys that have been conducted in OECD countries is provided in Chapter 3. Although the surveys differ in target audience, approach to measuring financial literacy, and survey methodology, one result common to them all is the low level of financial understanding and awareness among respondents.

Chapters 4-6 of this book discuss the importance of financial education for saving and investing for retirement, effectively using credit and debt, and bringing the unbanked into the financial system. Developments that have increased the importance of financial education are described, and selected financial education programmes are summarized, their effectiveness is evaluated and the implications for policymakers are explored. Chapter 7 presents the conclusions and some suggestions for future work in financial education.

Annexes A through D of the book provide additional information on the financial education programmes targeted to savers and investors for retirement, users of credit and debt, and the unbanked that are currently offered in OECD countries. Annex E contains a copy of the Recommendation on Principles and Good Practices for Financial Education and Awareness adopted by the OECD Council.

Acknowledgements

*I*mproving Financial Literacy: Analysis of Issues and Policies is the first major publication on financial education at the international level. It is the result of a collaborative effort on the part of the OECD Secretariat, delegates to the Committee on Financial Markets, and experts from many countries. It also benefited from the support and dedication of the Chairman of the Committee on Financial Markets, Lorenzo Bini Smaghi.

In the OECD Secretariat, a number of the staff of the Financial Affairs Division was involved in the production of this book. The publication was prepared under the direction of Barbara Smith, the manager of the Financial Education Project, who coordinated the research and wrote major sections of it. Philippa Michel Finch wrote the chapter on the unbanked and assisted with editing of other chapters while Joon Kyoon Lee wrote the chapter on credit. Research assistance was provided by Jean Marc Salou and Ayumi Kikuchi and technical and administrative support by Claire Dehouck, Sally Day, and Edward Smiley. The publication benefited also from significant contributions by Stephen Lumpkin and Gert Wehinger and from overall policy guidance by André Laboul, who also directly coordinated the work on the related OECD Recommendation.

The research for this book was conducted as part of the programme of work of the OECD's Financial Education Project, which has been supported by a grant from Prudential plc of the UK, an international financial services group that provides retail financial services and fund management to clients in the United Kingdom, the United States, Asia and continental Europe.*

---

* Projects on financial literacy form an integral part of Prudential's Corporate Responsibility programme. It is working in this area with a number of partners, including Citizens Advice, the Personal Finance Education Group (pfeg), National Institute for Adult Continuing Education (NIACE), the Specialist Schools and Academies Trust and local partners in China and Vietnam.

Table of Contents

IMPROVING FINANCIAL LITERACY – ISBN 92-64-01256-7 – © OECD 2005

List of boxes

List of tables

List of figures

ISBN 92-64-01256-7
Improving Financial Literacy
Analysis of Issues and Policies
© OECD 2005

Executive Summary

The importance of financial education has increased in recent years as a result of financial market developments and demographic, economic and policy changes. Financial markets are becoming more sophisticated and new products are continuously offered. Consumers now have greater access to a variety of credit and savings instruments provided by a range of entities from on-line banks and brokerage firms to community-based groups. As a result of changes in pension arrangements, an increasing number of workers will be assuming more responsibility for saving for their retirement. With the increase in life expectancy, individuals will need to ensure that they have adequate savings for the longer period they can expect to spend in retirement. These developments have important consequences for people saving or investing for retirement, for users of credit, and for the "unbanked", the three groups of consumers that are the focus of this study.

This book, the first major study of financial education at the international level, contributes to the development of consumer financial literacy by providing information to policymakers on effective financial education programmes and by facilitating the exchange of views and the sharing of experience in the field of financial education and awareness. The study identifies and analyses financial literacy surveys in member countries, highlights the economic, demographic and policy changes that make financial education increasingly important, describes the different types of financial education programmes currently being offered in OECD countries, evaluates their effectiveness to the extent possible, and suggests actions policymakers can take to improve financial education and awareness. This study presents the research that has been conducted to date by the OECD's Financial Education Project, established in 2003 in response to the increased importance of financial education in member countries.[1]

This book does not attempt to present a full accounting of all existing financial education programmes, a task which is beyond the scope of the Financial Education Project. Instead, it focuses on the major delivery channels, such as Web sites, brochures, courses, and media campaigns, and on the three financial issues identified by the responses to the OECD's questionnaires on financial education as important to member countries: investing and saving for retirement, handling credit and debt, and bringing the unbanked into the financial system.

These three issues were considered important by member countries for the following reasons:

- An increasing number of workers will have to rely on defined contribution pensions and their personal savings to finance their retirement as governments begin scaling back the benefits of state-supported social security programmes and as the number of employers offering defined benefit plans decreases.

- Consumer debt has been increasing to all-time high levels and the deregulation of financial markets has led to increased competition for new credit card holders. As a result, many young people have been burdened with high debts at a time when they are trying to start a family and buy a home.

- With the growth in the number of financial transactions taking place electronically, it is increasingly important that individuals have at least a bank account. Yet in a number of countries a significant percentage of consumers do not participate in the financial system. This percentage is even higher for minority consumers.

This book focuses on programmes that are offered outside of schools. Research for the current report indicates, however, that it is important to educate individuals as early as possible about financial issues. Consequently, the next stage of the project, to be developed in cooperation with the Education Committee, would describe and analyse financial education programmes available in schools and universities. This second stage of the project is expected to result in a major report on financial literacy among young people and the state of financial education in schools.

The OECD will also develop further work on financial education and awareness with respect to insurance and pensions. The research in the book report will be extended to examine in more detail the important role of financial education in increasing consumers' awareness and understanding of insurance issues, including the benefits of insurance coverage. Another extension of the research presented in this book will focus on the role of financial education in both defined benefit and defined contribution pension schemes and the development of appropriate guidelines on financial education for retirement savings.

Factors increasing the importance of financial education

- *The complexity of financial products.* Consumers are now faced with a variety of different types of financial instruments offering a range of options with respect to fees, interest rates, maturities, etc. The quality of some of these financial products, such as life insurance policies, is difficult to assess because they are purchased infrequently and there is often a significant lapse of time between purchase and use.

- *Increase in the number of financial products.* Deregulation of financial markets and the reduction in costs brought about by developments in information technology and telecommunications have resulted in a proliferation in the number of new products tailored to meet very specific market needs. The Internet has also increased both the amount of information about investment and credit products and the availability of these products.

- *The baby boom and increases in life expectancy.* Many OECD countries experienced a baby boom after the Second World War. The first of these baby boomers will begin retiring over the next five to ten years. As many baby boomers delayed childbearing or chose to have fewer children or none at all, the cohorts following the baby boom are much smaller. Thus, the retirement of the baby boom generation means that there will be fewer workers supporting a greater number of retirees. The situation is further compounded by the increase in life expectancy, which means that this large cohort might be spending more time in retirement than previous generations and might, therefore, need to be supported for a longer time. The aging of the populations in OECD countries will have severe consequences for pay-as-you-go public retirement programmes.

- *Changes in pension arrangements.* A major trend in pension systems in the OECD countries is the shift from defined benefit to defined contribution pension schemes. In the former, the pension provider guarantees a set retirement income, while in the latter it is the contribution levels that are set, with the retirement income depending upon the contribution rates and the investment decisions made during the individual's work life. As a result, more of the risk in pension provisioning is shifted from the provider to the worker. In the future, an increasing number of retirees will depend upon income from defined contribution pension plans.

- *Low levels of financial literacy.* A review of financial literacy surveys in twelve OECD countries concluded that financial understanding among consumers is low. Financial literacy levels are especially low for certain groups, such as the less-educated, minorities, and those at the lower end of the income distribution.

*Benefits of financial education to consumers
and the economy*

Financial education can benefit consumers of all ages and income levels. For young adults just beginning their working lives, it can provide basic tools for budgeting and saving so that expenses and debt can be kept under control. Financial education can help families acquire the discipline to save for a home of their own and/or for their children's education. It can help older workers ensure that they have enough savings for a comfortable retirement by providing them with the information and skills to make wise investment choices with both their pension plans and any individual savings plans. Financial education can help those at low income levels make the most of what they are able to save and help them avoid the high cost charged for financial transactions by non-financial institution such as check cashing services. For those consumers with money to invest, financial education can provide increased understanding of both basic financial information, such as the trade-off between risk and return and the value of compound interest, as well as more specific information about the advantages and disadvantages of particular types of investments.

Financially educated consumers can also benefit the economy. By demanding products more responsive to their needs, they also encourage providers to develop new products and services, thus increasing competition in financial markets, innovation and improvement in quality. Financially educated consumers are also more likely to save and to save more than their less literate counterparts. The increase in savings associated with greater financial literacy should have positive effects on both investment levels and economic growth. In emerging economies, providing both information and training to consumers on the operation of markets and on the roles of market participants can help these countries make the most of their developing markets. In addition, financially educated consumers are in a better position to protect themselves on their own and to report possible misconducts by financial intermediaries to the authorities. Thus, they would facilitate supervisory activity and might in principle allow for lower levels of regulatory intervention. As a result, there would be reduced regulatory burden on firms.

Definition of financial education

As this is the first major international study on financial education, the definition of what constitutes financial education is intentionally kept broad. By using a broad definition of financial education that includes elements of information, instruction, and advice, this report is as inclusive and comprehensive as possible in the identification, description, and analysis of financial education programmes.

Financial education is the process by which financial consumers/investors improve their understanding of financial products and concepts and, through information, instruction and/or objective advice, develop the skills and confidence to become more aware of financial risks and opportunities, to make informed choices, to know where to go for help, and to take other effective actions to improve their financial well-being.

Where:

- *information* involves providing consumers with facts, data, and specific knowledge to make them aware of financial opportunities, choices, and consequences;

- *instruction* involves ensuring that individuals acquire the skills and ability to understand financial terms and concepts, through the provision of training and guidance; and

- *advice* involves providing consumers with counsel about generic financial issues and products so that they can make the best use of the financial information and instruction they have received.[2]

Finally, financial education also needs to be distinguished from consumer protection, although there is some overlap between the two.[3] The provision of information on financial issues is common to both. However, financial education supplements this information with the provision of instruction and advice while consumer protection emphasises legislation and regulation designed to enforce minimum standards, require financial institutions to provide clients with appropriate information, strengthen the legal protection of consumers when something goes wrong, and provide for systems of redress.

Provision of financial education

The most frequently used way of providing financial education is through publications. These publications take a variety of forms including brochures, magazines, booklets, guidance papers, newsletters, annual reports, direct mail documents, letters and disclosure documents. Another often used method is the Internet, in the form of Web sites, Web portals, and other online services. Other methods used include advisory services, including telephone help lines; public educational campaigns and events, including presentations, lectures, conferences, symposia; and training courses and seminars and other types of channel, such as CD ROMs and videos, etc. The providers of financial education can be the public (or semi-public) sector: government agencies, ministries (of finance and social affairs, for example), central banks, and regulatory and supervisory authorities. Private sector providers of financial education include consumers' and employees' associations as well financial institutions. While many programmes are intended for consumers in general, some are targeted to specific groups, such as women, minorities, or those with low-incomes.

Summary of report findings

- Countries are increasingly aware of the importance of financial education, providing a variety of financial education programmes and initiatives, ranging from websites, to distribution of brochures and pamphlets on selected financial issues, to offering of training courses or conducting media campaigns. Some countries have given considerable thought to evaluating financial education programmes and to identifying the characteristics of effective financial education programmes. A few countries consider financial education so important that they are developing national strategies to coordinate and direct their financial education programmes.

- Countries also provide financial education on a wide range of issues, including credit, insurance, investment and pensions. Much of this information is directed to the general public although some of it is targeted more specifically to investors, consumers burdened with debt, or those individuals outside of the financial system. However, it is not clear to what extent the financial information presented to consumers takes into account the variability across consumers in financial understanding.

- Few countries have undertaken nationally representative financial literacy surveys to determine the financial issues that are of most concern and create a need for increased competence among consumers. The surveys that have been undertaken indicate that many consumers do not have an adequate financial background or understanding and that they often overestimate their knowledge of financial issues. The surveys that ask questions about consumer demographics find that financial understanding is correlated with education and income levels, although highly educated consumers with high incomes can be just as ignorant about financial issues as less educated, lower income consumers. These surveys also indicate that consumers have difficulty in finding and understanding financial information.

- There have been relatively few evaluations of financial education programmes to determine what has worked well and what has not. This is, in part, due to the fact that programme evaluation is expensive and government budgets are limited. Equally important, however, is the difficulty of devising feasible measures to assess whether the main goals of financial education programmes-increasing consumer awareness and changing individual financial behaviour-have been fulfilled. When financial information is provided through websites or brochures distributed in public places, it is difficult to develop effective measures of behaviour change. For example, what indicators could researchers use to determine if who accessed a website or picked up a brochure understood what they read and/or changed their behaviour as a result?

- Where evaluated, financial education programmes have been found to be effective. Research in the United States shows that workers increase their participation in and contributions to 401(k) plans when employers offer financial education, whether in the form of brochures or seminars. Financial education in the form of mortgage counselling has been found to be effective in reducing the risk of mortgage delinquency. Consumers who attend one on one credit counselling sessions have lower debt and fewer delinquencies than consumers who do not. More subjective evaluations of financial education programmes for the unbanked have found that participants are satisfied with the training they received and are more confident about making financial decisions.

- Financial education programmes might not always be the only effective approach to improving consumer well being. In certain circumstances other approaches might be needed either as a complement to or a substitute for financial education. Research in behavioural finance has shown, for example, that psychological traits, such as inertia and lack of willpower, might reduce the effectiveness of financial education programmes. This has led some experts to argue for automatic enrolment for defined contribution plans along with default contribution rates and default asset allocation. However, these alternative approaches also have their critics. Automatic enrolment, for example, has been criticized for low contribution rates and conservative asset allocations. Therefore, most experts also acknowledge that financial education still has a role to play in providing advice and information to workers about their retirement plans.

- Based on the results of this study, the representatives of the 30 member governments of the OECD developed a Recommendation on Principles and Good Practices for Financial Education and Awareness. The good practices include suggestions on how governments can increase both public awareness of financial issues and the dissemination of financial information, on how financial institutions can provide objective and unbiased information on financial products, on the role of employers in the provision of financial information on retirement saving, and on the issues providers need to consider in determining the content and delivery of financial education programmes.

What remains to be done

What the research for this book makes clear, however, is that there is much more to do and learn about financial education programmes and how to make them better. First, it is important to increase consumer awareness as to the necessity of financial education and how they can access it. Financial education is not just for investors. It is just as important, if not more so, for the average family trying to balance its budget and save for the children's education and the parent's retirement. More needs to be learned about the financial education needs of consumers at various stages in their lives and how financial education programmes can be designed and implemented to best address these needs. How can financial education programmes better reach those consumers who most need them? More needs to be learned about how consumers prefer to receive information on financial issues. How can financial education programmes be best delivered to consumers busy with jobs and families? Objective measures identifying programme success need to be developed and more evaluations of programmes need to be conducted. Ideally, more information needs to be gathered on individual programmes in order to more confidently produce a list of good practices. More research and more evaluation are necessary. Currently it is not possible to compare financial literacy either across countries or over time within a country. In addition, data on savings rates, household debt, and changes in pension coverage are difficult to find in the detail necessary to allow a critical comparison across countries. Further research is necessary to ensure that all consumers are provided with effective financial information and education.

Notes

1. This part of the Financial Education Project is designed and carried out under the supervision of the Committee on Financial Markets. The project was made possible by generous funding from Prudential plc.

2. Specifically excluded are programmes that offer recommandations regarding individual financial products and services, for example, advice recommanding the purchase of financial product X offered by financial institution Y.

3. Although financial education provides policymakers with another tool for promoting economic growth, confidence, and stability, and as such should be taken into account in the regulatory framework, it is not meant to be a substitute for, but rather a complement to, financial regulation or other consumer protection legislation.

ISBN 92-64-01256-7
Improving Financial Literacy
Analysis of Issues and Policies
© OECD 2005

Chapter 1

Overview of Report

Financial education has always been important for consumers in helping them budget and manage their income, save and invest efficiently, and avoid becoming victims of fraud. However, as financial markets become increasingly sophisticated and as households assume more of the responsibility and risk for financial decisions, financial education is increasingly necessary for individuals, not only to ensure their own financial well-being, but also to facilitate the smooth functioning of financial markets and the economy. By creating demand for products more responsive to their needs, financially literate consumers encourage providers to develop new products and services, thus increasing competition in financial markets, with a resulting increase in innovation and improvement in quality. Financial markets that are operating efficiently and expanding will help to foster economic growth. In addition, financial education has been shown to increase both the number of individuals with savings and the average amount of savings, which should have important impacts on investment levels and economic growth.

This book, the first major study of financial education at the international level, contributes to the development of consumer financial literacy by providing information to policymakers on effective financial education programmes and by facilitating the exchange of views and the sharing of experience in the field of financial education and awareness.[1] It identifies and analyses financial literacy surveys in member countries, highlights the economic, demographic and policy changes that make financial education increasingly important, describes the different types of financial education programmes currently being offered in OECD countries, evaluates their effectiveness to the extent possible, and suggests actions policymakers can take to improve financial education and awareness. This book presents the research that has been conducted to date by the OECD's Financial Education Project, established in 2003 in response to the increased importance of financial education in member countries.[2]

Definition of financial education

As this is the first major international study on financial education, the definition of what constitutes financial education is intentionally kept broad. By using a broad definition of financial education that includes elements of information, instruction, and advice, this report is as inclusive and comprehensive as possible in the identification, description, and analysis of financial education programmes.

IMPROVING FINANCIAL LITERACY – ISBN 92-64-01256-7 – © OECD 2005

Financial education is the process by which financial consumers/investors improve their understanding of financial products and concepts and, through information, instruction and/or objective advice, develop the skills and confidence to become more aware of financial risks and opportunities, to make informed choices, to know where to go for help, and to take other effective actions to improve their financial well-being.

Where:

- *information* involves providing consumers with facts, data, and specific knowledge to make them aware of financial opportunities, choices, and consequences;

- *instruction* involves ensuring that individuals acquire the skills and ability to understand financial terms and concepts, through the provision of training and guidance; and

- *advice* involves providing consumers with counsel about generic financial issues and products so that they can make the best use of the financial information and instruction they have received.[3]

Finally, financial education also needs to be distinguished from consumer protection, although there is some overlap between the two.[4] Consumer protection and financial education share many of the same goals but each takes a somewhat different approach. Both financial education and consumer protection have as aims to ensure the well-being of consumers and to shield them from harm. The provision of information on financial issues is common to both. However, financial education supplements this information with the provision of instruction and advice while consumer protection emphasises legislation and regulation designed to enforce minimum standards, require financial institutions to provide clients with appropriate information, strengthen the legal protection of consumers when something goes wrong, and provide for systems of redress. In other words, consumer protection puts the burden on the financial institutions and the legal system whereas with financial education the burden is on the individual.

Financial education and consumer protection are not substitutes but rather complements. The latter provides a safety net for those consumers who are unable or unwilling to improve their financial education. It is important for both consumer well-being and for the effective operation of financial markets that consumers have full knowledge of the range of products available and of various contractual rights and obligations. Some consumers can acquire this knowledge through financial education programmes. However, others may be either unable or unwilling to do so and for these individuals consumer protection is important. In addition, because the fitness or unfitness of financial products may not be known for years, consumer protection can benefit all consumers by ensuring that they not only know what they are getting when they purchase a financial product but also that it is a product suitable for their needs.

Methodology

Two approaches were used to identify information on financial literacy and education. The first approach consisted of circulating four questionnaires to the national authorities of OECD member countries. These questionnaires asked about the important issues in financial education, the main obstacles to providing financial education, the major financial education initiatives underway, the existence of surveys of financial literacy, evaluations of the effectiveness of financial education programmes, and specific financial, policy and demographic developments making the provision of financial education increasingly important. Much country specific information, including details on financial literacy surveys, was received this way.

The second approach involved an extensive literature review of relevant studies in economics, social policy and related fields. Evaluations of existing financial education programmes were identified through this approach and reviewed to determine the factors contributing to the effectiveness of these programmes. The literature review also provided additional information on economic, policy and demographic developments to complement that received through the questionnaires.

Limitations

As noted earlier, this book is not intended to be a complete catalogue of all existing financial education programmes. Identifying these programmes would be a massive undertaking. Financial education programmes are offered by the public as well as by the private sector. In the public sector, such programmes are offered at all levels of government, from the national level down to the local level. In the private sector, many small, non-profit community groups offer financial education programmes. Community-based financial education programmes are offered by universities and by financial institutions. In addition, these programmes are offered in a variety of languages. Because this field is quite new, it was not always clear to the governments receiving the OECD's questionnaires on financial education to which agency they should forward them. As a result, responses were received from Financial Ministries, Central Banks, and Education Ministries, as well as from consumer protection agencies.

It was also difficult for the reasons noted above to find as much detail as would be desirable on many of the programmes. Details on target audience, number of individuals served, the costs of programmes, the goals of the programme, or on objective measures of success are not available for many programmes. Therefore, it is impossible in these cases to provide an evaluation of the effectiveness of the financial education programmes described in this report. Even where more details on programmes are available, the characteristics of the delivery channel will affect the extent to

22

which a programme can be evaluated. For example, it would be difficult to determine the effectiveness of websites or of brochures. Although there might be information on the number of Web site hits or the number of brochures distributed, there would be no way to know if the information provided in the Web site or brochures had been read, understood, and acted upon.

Organisation of the report

The next chapter highlights the increasing importance of financial education, its contributions to market efficiency and consumer well-being, and the role of financial intermediaries. Here the book discusses briefly the developments affecting the importance of financial education, such as the increase in the number and complexity of financial products, the baby boom and increases in life expectancy, changes in pension arrangements, and the low level of consumer financial literacy.

The third chapter describes six financial literacy surveys for which there is detailed information on methodology, results, questions asked, and target groups. Despite the differences across surveys, all conclude that financial literacy of consumers is low. This review concludes with some implications of these surveys for the design and implementation of financial education programmes.

Chapters 4, 5 and 6, discuss the importance of financial education for, respectively, saving and investing for retirement, effectively using credit and debt, and bringing the unbanked into the financial system. In each case, there is a description of the developments leading to the increased importance of financial education in the particular are in question, a summary of selected financial education programmes in this area, and an evaluation of the effectiveness of these programmes, which includes a discussion of the implications for policymakers. Chapter 7 presents the conclusions and some suggestions for future work in financial education.

Annexes A through D of the book provide additional information on the financial education programmes targeted to savers and investors for retirement, users of credit and debt, and the unbanked that are currently offered in OECD countries. Annex E contains a copy of the Recommendation on Principles and Good Practices for Financial Education and Awareness adopted by the OECD Council. Annex E contains a copy of this Recommendation.

Notes

1. The Financial Education Project at the OECD is also developing an inventory of financial education programmes in member countries. In addition, a Web page (*www.oecd.org/daf/financialeducation*) has been set up and there are plans to create an electronic discussion group and organise conferences in order to facilitate communication and the exchange of information on financial education issues.

2. This part of the Financial Education Project is designed and carried out under the supervision of the Committee on Financial Markets. The project was made possible by generous funding from Prudential plc.

3. Specifically excluded are programmes that offer recommendations regarding individual financial products and services, for example, advice recommending the purchase of financial product X offered by financial institution Y.

4. Although financial education provides policymakers with another tool for promoting economic growth, confidence, and stability, and as such should be taken into account in the regulatory framework, it is not meant to be a substitute for, but rather a complement to, financial regulation or other consumer protection legislation.

ISBN 92-64-01256-7
Improving Financial Literacy
Analysis of Issues and Policies
© OECD 2005

Chapter 2

Financial Education:
Its Definition, its Increasing Importance,
its Contributions to Market Efficiency
and Consumer Well-being,
and the Role of Financial Intermediaries

Definition of financial education

As this is the first major international study on financial education, the definition of what constitutes financial education is intentionally kept broad. By using a broad definition of financial education that includes elements of information, instruction, and advice, this report is as inclusive and comprehensive as possible in the identification, description, and analysis of financial education programmes.

Financial education is the process by which financial consumers/investors improve their understanding of financial products and concepts and, through information, instruction and/or objective advice, develop the skills and confidence to become more aware of financial risks and opportunities, to make informed choices, to know where to go for help, and to take other effective actions to improve their financial well-being.

Where:

- *information* involves providing consumers with facts, data, and specific knowledge to make them aware of financial opportunities, choices, and consequences;

- *instruction* involves ensuring that individuals acquire the skills and ability to understand financial terms and concepts, through the provision of training and guidance; and

- *advice* involves providing consumers with counsel about generic financial issues and products so that they can make the best use of the financial information and instruction they have received.[1]

Finally, financial education also needs to be distinguished from consumer protection, although there is some overlap between the two.[2] Consumer protection and financial education share many of the same goals but each takes a somewhat different approach. Both financial education and consumer protection have as aims to ensure the well-being of consumers and to shield them from harm. The provision of information on financial issues is common to both. However, financial education supplements this information with the provision of instruction and advice while consumer protection emphasises legislation and regulation designed to enforce minimum standards, require financial institutions to provide clients with appropriate information, strengthen the legal protection of consumers when something goes wrong, and provide for systems of redress.

Financial education and consumer protection are not substitutes but rather complements. The latter provides a safety net for those consumers who are unable or unwilling to improve their financial literacy. It is important for both consumer well-being and for the effective operation of financial markets that consumers have full knowledge of the range of products available and of various contractual rights and obligations. Some consumers can acquire this knowledge through financial education programmes. However, others may be either unable or unwilling to do so and for these individuals consumer protection is important. In addition, because the fitness or unfitness of financial products may not be known for years, consumer protection can benefit all consumers by ensuring that they not only know what they are getting when they purchase a financial product but also that it is a product suitable for their needs.

The increasing importance of financial education

The importance of financial education has increased in recent years as a result of financial market developments and demographic, economic and policy changes. Financial markets are becoming more sophisticated and new products are continuously offered. Consumers now have greater access to a variety of credit and savings instruments provided by a range of entities, from on-line banks and brokerage firms to community based groups. As a result of changes in pension arrangements, an increasing number of workers will be assuming more responsibility for saving for their retirement. With the increase in life expectancy, individuals will need to ensure that they have adequate savings for the longer period they can expect to spend in retirement. These developments have important consequences for people saving or investing for retirement, for users of credit, and for the "unbanked", the three groups of consumers that are the focus of this report.

As a result of the developments mentioned above, an increasing number of consumers in OECD countries are actively participating in financial markets. Some of these consumers are first-time investors in well-established markets in which the investment products are constantly changing. Others are first-time investors in markets that themselves are very new. Other consumers are taking out loans or signing up for credit cards. Still others are opening bank accounts for the first time. The variety and complexity of financial products offered in today's financial markets, whether for investment, savings, credit or debt, can be challenging even for those with some basic financial knowledge. It can be completely overwhelming for those with little or no financial knowledge. Yet individuals in many countries now have to make more financial decisions and to take more responsibility for these decisions. At the same time, many of these individuals have had little preparation for the financial responsibilities which they now confront. Consequently, it is imperative that consumers become better educated regarding financial matters.

The consequence of the developments discussed in this chapter is that risk is being shifted, at least in part, from governments and financial institutions to households. This shift is seen most clearly in the switch from defined benefit to defined contribution pension plans. With the shift to defined contribution plans, retirement benefits will be increasingly funded by investments in capital markets and, thus, will be increasingly affected by movements in the prices of financial assets. Under defined contribution plans, individuals face a number of financial risks: investment risk during the accumulation phase and longevity and inflation risk during the decumulation phase. Individuals also face a high risk of volatility with the adequacy of retirement income dependent upon financial conditions in the year of retirement. The concern is that households may be neither aware of nor capable of managing these risks. Households are most likely to have only a limited experience with investing – perhaps a mortgage or a mutual fund, etc. However, even if they are aware of the risks, they might lack the financial understanding necessary to appreciate how these risks could affect them. Indeed, surveys of financial literacy in a number of countries indicate that many consumers do not have an adequate financial background or understanding. Thus, it is imperative that households be made aware that they will be increasingly bearing risks once borne by professional investors. They will need to be provided with information, advice, and assistance to help them manage these risks.

Factors making financial education increasingly important

The complexity of financial products

A generation ago most consumers had just two basic banking products: a checking account and a savings account. Such accounts were simple to open and maintain. Now, however, consumers are faced with a variety of different types of checking or bank accounts: accounts with fees that pay interest, accounts with no fees and no interest, accounts with no fees but a limit on the number of transactions per month, accounts with overdraft protection, etc., that may be provided by a number of different types of financial institutions. Consumers also have the choice among a number of savings vehicles: money market accounts, certificates of deposit, and a variety of other products with differing maturities and yields. For those individuals interested in investing in equities there are innovative products such as equity portfolios that enable an investor to purchase a complete portfolio of stocks with a single transaction but to trade the securities individually, at any time. Investors can also choose to invest in a variety of mutual funds, including international funds, growth funds, income funds, and tax-free funds. With respect to bonds, there are government bonds, municipal bonds, corporate bonds, and callable bonds, which are structured so that they can be retired by the issuer at specific dates and prices prior to maturity.

Even relatively straightforward financial products can appear quite complex to the average consumer, as they often require an understanding of terms to maturity, durations, payout options, and various other features. In addition, it is often difficult to assess the quality of financial products at the time of purchase. For example, with life insurance policies or pensions, it might be thirty years or more before the quality is known. Furthermore, as these products are purchased infrequently, there is limited scope for learning about quality from repeated purchases. Consequently, financial products can be difficult to understand and many consumers purchase inappropriate ones or decide not to purchase any at all.

Increase in the number of financial products

Deregulation of financial markets and the reduction in costs brought about by developments in information technology and telecommunications have resulted in a proliferation in the number of new products tailored to meet very specific market needs. These innovations in financial products and services have enabled more consumers to gain access to a greater variety of financial products. The Internet has also increased both the amount of information about investment and credit products and the availability of these products. The diversity of new financial products provides consumers with more choices but also more challenges.

Investors in equities, for example, now have access to many new trading mechanisms and venues, some of which offer speedier executions or greater anonymity, as well as access to many different types of investments. Users of credit and debt in many OECD countries are being presented with many new options for loans, credit cards, and other forms of debt. Technology has enabled a reduction in creditor costs through credit-scoring techniques and as a result more consumers have become eligible for credit. The unbanked, those who have no formal relationship with a financial institution, risk becoming even further isolated by recent changes in financial markets. With more financial decisions facing consumers and with an increased number of transactions assuming the existence or ownership of a bank account, those individuals without one or with limited use of one are increasingly at a disadvantage.

The baby boom and increases in life expectancy

Many OECD countries experienced a baby boom after the Second World War. The first of these baby boomers will begin retiring over the next five to ten years. As many baby boomers delayed childbearing or chose to have fewer children or none at all, the cohorts following the baby boom are much smaller. Thus, the retirement of the baby boom generation means that there will be fewer workers supporting a greater number of retirees. The situation is further compounded by the increase in life expectancy, which means that this large cohort of retirees might be spending more time in retirement than previous generations and might, therefore, need to be supported for a longer time.

The effects of this demographic change are clearly shown in the following figure, which presents old-age dependency ratios for selected countries in 2005, 2030 and 2050. The old age dependency ratio is defined as the number of people aged 65 or over divided by the number of people aged 15 to 64. This ratio will begin to increase in all the countries shown when the baby boom generation begins to retire. For the countries shown in Figure 2.1, the increase will be greatest for Italy and Japan and smallest for the United States. In Europe the old age dependency ratio is projected to increase from .23 in 2005 to .37 in 2030. This means that whereas in Europe there are currently four workers supporting each retiree, in 2030 there will be fewer than three. In Japan the old age dependency ratio is projected to increase from .30 in 2005 to .53 in 2030. This means that in 2030 there will be fewer than two workers supporting each retiree compared to three currently. It is evident from the figure that providing income for the aged will be a major problem for many countries.

Figure 2.1. **Old-age dependency ratios (65+ to 15-64), 2005, 2030 and 2050**

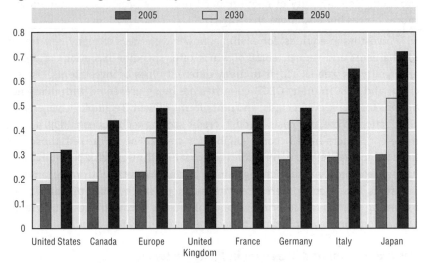

Source: United Nations (2003), *World Population Prospects: The 2002 Revision Population Database*, United Nations, New York.

The ageing of the populations in OECD countries will have severe consequences for pay-as-you-go public retirement programmes. The working population will not be large enough to support the ever growing number of retirees without changes to these programmes. Governments, in order to sustain these programmes, will face difficult choices such as cuts in benefits, tax increases, massive borrowing, lower cost-of-living adjustments, later retirement ages, or a combination of these elements. For individuals, the increase in life expectancy means the possibility of more time spent in retirement and, thus, a greater need for asset management, tax and estate planning, expanded insurance products, and other financial strategies as longevity increases.

The ageing of the baby boom generation might also have an adverse affect on the return to private savings (FRBSF, 1998). This effect could have serious repercussions because the baby boom generation will have to rely more heavily on personal savings for retirement income than did earlier generations. Holding other things constant, asset prices might be expected to fall when the large baby boom cohorts begin to sell their assets to the smaller cohorts that follow them.[3] However, this result is far from certain and expert opinion is divided as to what to expect. Several factors might mitigate the negative effect on asset prices. For example, if baby boomers decide to work longer, staying in the labour force beyond the traditional age of retirement, they would have less need to sell their assets as they would continue to receive earnings from their employment. Also, the baby boom generation is not expected to retire all at once, but rather over a period spanning 30 years. This period might be long enough to give capital markets time to adjust to the gradual decline in funds for capital investment. In addition, the younger cohorts following the baby boom, anticipating further cuts in benefits provided by pay-as-you-go schemes, might save a greater proportion of their incomes and thus this increased saving would compensate fro their smaller numbers. Given the potential impact, however, individuals need to be made aware of these uncertainties and the implications of these uncertainties for retirement savings.

Changes in pension arrangements

Investment decisions affecting retirement are the most important long-term financial decisions that many workers will have to make, and due to the increase in defined contribution plans, the responsibility for making these financial decisions is shifting more and more from the employer to the worker. Many defined contribution plans require that workers make decisions about whether to contribute, how much to contribute, and how to allocate these contributions across investment options. Workers also need to consider the different types of commissions that providers charge for investment and retirement. Additionally, defined contribution plans often require employees to choose among a range of financial products at retirement, some of which provide regular payments until death (annuities), while others involve gradual drawdown of the accumulated balance. Consequently, workers need to consider not only investment risks and returns but also uncertainty regarding their life expectancy as well as attitudes toward risk, current and future earnings potential, and any likely changes in personal circumstances.

The role of financial education programmes in providing assistance to workers will vary depending upon the characteristics of the defined contribution pension plan. In countries that have introduced mandatory defined contribution plans, such as those in Eastern Europe, there is often no individual choice of investment and very limited choices regarding retirement products and commission/fee structures. However, in countries such as Ireland, the United Kingdom, and the United States, which offer voluntary defined contribution plans, individuals need to make choices about participation, contribution, and asset allocation. The mandatory funded plans in Sweden and Australia also have investment choice, while in Hungary, portfolio choice has been available for voluntary pension savings since 2003. In those defined contribution plans offering participants a high degree of choice, financial education could be very helpful. Financial education is important as well for participants in defined benefit plans, for example with respect to portability.

Finally, pension reforms, in some cases, have been imposed on a population lacking a general understanding of the structure of the pension system and a personal awareness of individual pension entitlements and the role and responsibilities they have under the new pension regime. These individuals need to be given information not only regarding the basics of investing but also on why pension reform is necessary and what they can expect under the new system. As an example, in 2004 the government of the Slovak Republic initiated a ten-month media campaign – consisting of television ads, radio interviews and print advertising – to educate the public about the pension reforms that were scheduled to take place in January of 2005 (Jurinovà, 2004). A survey at the end of 2004 indicated that 80 per cent of respondents were aware of the information campaign and that almost 60 per cent approved of the reform (The Slovak Spectator, 2004).

Changes in income

The accumulation of financial assets by the baby boom generation resulted in a rise in the number of individual investors in many countries. Another factor explaining the increase in the number of individual investors is the rise in personal income that occurred in many countries over the past decade with the result that more people now have funds to invest.[4] Table 2.1 presents growth rates of per capita income in Canada, the European Union, and the United States. It shows that the growth of per capita income accelerated in the latter half of the 1990s. This acceleration represents a break with the slower growth of per capita income in the previous two decades.

Table 2.1. **Growth rates of per capita income**

	Canada	European Union	United States
1990-95	0.3	1.0	1.4
1995-2000	2.2	2.3	3.1

Source: B. van Ark (2002), "Understanding Productivity and Income Differentials Among OECD Countries: A Survey", *Review of Economic Performance and Social Progress*, Vol. 2, Institute for Research on Public Policy, Montreal.

As a result of this growth in income, there has been an increase in both the percentage of households investing as well as an increase in the amount of household wealth. The proportion of households investing directly or indirectly in stocks increased significantly in the 1990s for the countries shown in Table 2.2 below. Of note is the importance of investment through financial intermediaries, *e.g.* mutual funds and retirement accounts. When such indirect holdings are counted, the percentage of households investing in stocks more than doubles in most of the countries illustrated in the table. For example, in 1998, 19 per cent of American households had direct holdings of stocks; however, almost 49 per cent of households held stock either directly or indirectly. Increases in income also mean that more individuals can afford to make larger purchases on credit, to take out loans, and to buy homes.

Table 2.2. **Proportion of households investing in stocks**

	Direct stockholding (%)					Direct and indirect stockholding (%)				
	United States	United Kingdom	Netherlands	Germany	Italy	United States	United Kingdom	Netherlands	Germany	Italy
1983	19.1	8.9	–	9.7	–	–	–	–	11.2	–
1989	16.8	22.6	–	10.3	4.5	31.6	–	–	12.4	10.5
1995	15.2	23.4	11.5	10.5	4.0	40.4	–	29.4	15.6	14.0
1998	19.2	21.6	15.4	–	7.3	48.9	31.4	35.1	–	18.7

Direct stockholding: shares held directly.
Direct and indirect stockholding: Shares held directly, mutual funds, investment accounts, retirement accounts. With the exception of the US, information on the specific types of mutual funds and investment accounts is not available and thus it is not possible to disentangle indirect stockholding in mutual funds and managed investment accounts from investment in other financial assets. For this reason the reported figures overestimate the true value of indirect stockholding. In Germany there is no information on pension funds.
Source: L. Guiso, *et al.* (2000), "Household Portfolios: An International Compariosn", *Working Paper*, No. 48, Cento Studi in Economia e Finanza (Center for Studies in Economics and Finance), Universita Degli Studi di Salerno.

As Table 2.3 indicates, net financial wealth as a per cent of nominal disposable income has grown significantly in the 1990s. Equities as a per cent of disposable income have more than doubled in a number of countries in the same period.

Table 2.3. **Household wealth**[1]

	1990	1995	2000
Canada			
Net financial wealth	177.5	222.2	242.7
of which: Equities	49.6	67.6	95.7
France			
Net financial wealth	169.9	195.0	302.4
of which: Equities	114.1	89.6	174.2
Germany[2]			
Net financial wealth	123.2	135.6	162.9
of which: Equities	30.4	42.4	75.0
Italy			
Net financial wealth	196.3	224.0	302.9
of which: Equities	46.0	46.5	151.5
Japan			
Net financial wealth	261.9	285.1	337.7
of which: Equities	51.7	43.4	38.6
United Kingdom			
Net financial wealth	214.1	281.3	375.5
of which: Equities	61.2	71.7	111.4
United States			
Net financial wealth	259.0	304.9	372.0
of which: Equities	52.1	97.7	148.6

1. Net financial wealth and equities expressed as per cent of nominal disposable income. Households include non-profit institutions serving households. Net financial wealth is defined as financial assets minus liabilities. Financial assets comprise currency and deposits, securities other than shares, loans, shares and other equity, insurance technical reserves; and other accounts receivable/payable. Not included are assets with regard to social security pension insurance schemes. Equities comprise shares and other equity, including quoted, unquoted and mutual fund shares.
2. The first column represents figures from 1991.
Source: OECD (2002), *OECD Economic Outlook*, No. 72, December, Annex Table 56, OECD, Paris.

Changes in capital markets

In addition, more consumers in countries with newly developing capital markets are becoming involved in financial markets. These consumers have limited experience with capital markets. In these countries there is often low awareness of financial products and services, distrust of modern financial instruments, and a belief in a traditional way of saving money. The level of financial literacy among individual investors in these countries is often very low and these investors risk suffering losses due to their insufficient knowledge of financial issues and of the risks of financial investments. Also, it is often difficult for these investors to find information and guidance. Financial education programmes will need to address the needs of these consumers, who will require basic information on the operation of financial markets as well as information on different types of investments and the risks they entail.

Contributions of financial education to financial markets, the economy and consumers

Contributions to financial markets and the economy

Financially educated consumers help increasingly complex financial markets to operate efficiently. By their greater ability to compare risk-return characteristics of different financial products offered by various intermediaries (as well as differing costs involved), financially literate consumers enhance competition. In addition, by demanding products more responsive to their needs, they also encourage providers to develop new products and services, thus increasing competition in financial markets, innovation and improvement in quality. Financially educated consumers are also more likely to save and to save more than their less literate counterparts.[5] The increase in savings associated with greater financial literacy should have positive effects on both investment levels and economic growth.

In addition, financial education can serve to augment and strengthen consumer protection. Financially educated consumers are in a better position to protect themselves on their own and to report possible misconducts by financial intermediaries to the authorities. As Alan Greenspan, chairman of the Board of Governors of the Federal Reserve System, has stated, educated consumers are "simply less vulnerable to fraud and abuse" (Greenspan, 2003b). Thus, financially educated consumers would facilitate supervisory activity and might in principle allow for lower levels of regulatory intervention. As a result, there would be reduced regulatory burden on firms. Governments would need to spend fewer resources on enforcement of regulations and on the investigation and prosecution of fraud.

In emerging economies, providing both information and training to consumers on the operation of markets and on the roles of market participants can help these countries make the most of their developing markets. Financially educated consumers can help ensure that the financial sector makes an effective contribution to real economic growth and poverty reduction. Further, financially well-educated consumers might be able to dampen swings in financial markets in that they are less likely to react prematurely, or to overreact, to external volatility because they have a better understanding of market conditions in their country.

Benefits of financial education to consumers

Financial education can benefit consumers of all ages and income levels. For young adults just beginning their working lives, it can provide basic tools for budgeting and saving so that expenses and debt can be kept under control. Financial education can help families acquire the discipline to save for a home of their own and/or for their children's education. It can help older workers ensure that they have enough savings for a comfortable retirement by providing them with the information and skills to make wise investment choices with both their pension plans and any individual savings plans. Financial education can help those at low income levels make the most of what they are able to save and help them avoid the high costs charged for financial transactions by non-financial institutions such as check cashing services. For those consumers with money to invest, financial education can provide increased understanding of both basic financial information, such as the trade-off between risk and return and the value of compound interest, as well as more specific information about the advantages and disadvantages of particular types of investments.

Consumers more than ever need a certain level of financial understanding in order to evaluate and compare the increasingly voluminous and complex information available on different financial products. Without a certain level of financial literacy, consumers might not purchase the financial products and services they need and/or might acquire unneeded or inappropriate financial products. Financial education can contribute to consumer well-being by helping them become better informed about financial products and services. Becoming financially better informed involves, first, acquiring information (i.e. determining where to find the information and getting hold of it) and, second, processing this information (i.e. understanding the information and using it to make better informed financial decisions, including those about investment and retirement savings). Rational consumers will acquire and process information as long as the marginal costs of doing so are less than the perceived marginal benefits of this information. Thus, reducing these costs will encourage consumers who have not already done so to seek information about investments and encourage those who already have some financial understanding of investment to acquire more. Financial education programmes can help reduce these costs by providing more information to consumers on investment products and services, thus making such information easier to find and acquire, and by helping consumers process this information and use it to make better informed decisions.

Role of financial intermediaries

In their ordinary activity, financial intermediaries may not always be in a position to provide financial education to the full extent of its meaning. Instead, as already prescribed by the regulations in place in many countries, financial intermediaries should have a responsibility to provide clients information that clearly and accurately represents the terms and conditions associated with the products they offer, openly describes the interests of the financial intermediary and its relationship to the information provided, and avoids deceptive language in marketing materials. By providing understandable and unbiased information and by being clear about their role in the process, financial intermediaries can strengthen the role of financial education, mainly by increasing individuals' awareness.

The provision of clear and accurate information by financial institutions will also enhance the competitive process by enabling market participants to know the risk-return characteristics to investment and, therefore, to decide where capital should flow. At the same time, it must also be recognized that financial intermediaries may as well benefit from improved financial literacy and education of customers since this facilitates the provision of accurate and appropriate financial information and advice.

In addition to providing financial information, financial intermediaries should make sure that consumers are aware of the financial services available and know how to access them. Some analysts have suggested that the responsibility of financial intermediaries should extend to the provision of training and that financial intermediaries have an obligation to ensure that consumers understand the information they provide. With regard to the latter, for example, the recently approved European Union Directive on Markets for Financial Instruments (MIFID) strengthens regulation already included in the previous 1993 Directive on Investment Services (ISD) requiring that the financial intermediary assess the financial situation of the consumer, determine the degree of risk the consumer is willing and able to take, and provide the consumer with all the information necessary to adequately judge the financial products and services offered. More generally, financial institutions should be encouraged to check that the information provided to their clients is read and understood, for instance through tests and especially for those financial services which entail long-term commitment or have potentially significant financial consequences.

A number of countries are considering regulations or legislation to improve the disclosure of information by financial intermediaries. For example, in Hong Kong, China, the Mandatory Provident Fund Schemes Authority is currently drafting a code on disclosure for investment funds that will provide scheme members with clearer and easier-to-understand information, enabling them to make more efficient investment decisions. A government working group in Finland has recommended that all investment fund companies and investment service suppliers be subject to uniform regulation so that consumers would have access to comparable information about the costs and risks of different long-term savings products.[6]

Many financial intermediaries support financial education initiatives. A 2005 Consumer Bankers Association survey in the United States finds that 96% of the banks surveyed either offered financial education programmes or worked with partners to support such efforts (CBA, 2005). Although some banks participate because they want to be recognised as good corporate citizens, others realise that these activities help them reach hard-to-serve markets such as immigrants or others without a relationship with a bank (Greenspan, 2003a).

Central banks can also play a role in the provision of financial education. For example, the Federal Reserve Board and the Reserve Banks in the United States are very active in promoting consumer education and financial literacy training. They work with financial institutions and community groups to highlight the importance of financial education and to increase consumer awareness of local financial educational opportunities. They are also encouraging research into finding the most effective approaches for educating the public about financial issues and for evaluating financial education programmes (Ferguson, 2002).

Notes

1. Specifically excluded are programmes that offer recommendations regarding individual financial products and services, for example, advice recommending the purchase of financial product X offered by financial institution Y.

2. Although financial education provides policymakers with another tool for promoting economic growth, confidence, and stability, and as such should be taken into account in the regulatory framework, it is not meant to be a substitute for, but rather a complement to, financial regulation or other consumer protection legislation.

3. This is the view expressed by the "asset meltdown" hypothesis.

4. Although income has increased, there is a range of attitudes among consumers toward saving and spending. People know they should save; however, they often give in to the desire for immediate gratification. Research in the US has found that a certain percentage of consumers are dedicated savers who think that individuals should take responsibility for their retirement. However, a much larger percentage of consumers have a "live for today" attitude and prefer to spend money than to save it. It is this latter group that would especially benefit from financial education (MacFarland et al., 2003). Such consumers are likely to start saving too late in life and save too little to achieve the goal of a comfortable retirement income. Financial education might help these consumers appreciate the need for asset management, tax and estate planning, expanded insurance products, and other financial strategies increases.

5. Studies have shown that financial education programmes increase both the number of individuals who save and the average amount of their savings (Bayer, et al., 1996; Clark and Schieber, 1998; and Lusardi, 2003).

6. Responses to OECD's questionnaire on financial education sent to delegates of the Committee on Financial Markets.

References

Bayer, P., D. Bernheim and K. Scholz (1996), "The Effects of Financial Education in the Workplace: Evidence from a Survey of Employers", *Working Paper*, No. 5655, National Bureau of Economic Research.

Clark, R. and S. Schieber (1998) "Factors Affecting Participation Rates and Contribution Levels in 401(k) Plans", in O. Mitchell and S. Schieber (eds.), *Living with Defined Contribution Plans*, University of Pennsylvania Press, Philadelphia.

Consumer Bankers Association (CBA) (2005), *2005 Survey of Bank-Sponsored Financial Literacy Programs*, *www.cbanet.org*, accessed 26 July 2005.

Federal Reserve Bank of San Francisco (FRBSF) (1998), "The Baby Boom, the Baby Bust, and Asset Markets", *FRBSF Economic Letter*, 98-20, 26 June, *www.frbsf.org/econrsrch/wklyltr/wklyltr98/el98-20.html*, accessed 2 February 2005.

Ferguson, R. (2002), *Reflections on Financial Literacy*, Remarks, National Council on Economic Education, Washington D.C., 13 May, *www.federalreserve.gov/boarddocs/speeches/2002/20020513/default.com*, accessed 4 January 2004.

Greenspan, A. (2003a), *Financial Education*, Remarks, 33rd Annual Legislative Conference of the Congressional Black Caucus, Washington D.C., 26 September, *www.federalreserve.gov/boarddocs/speeches/2003/20030926/default.htm*, accessed 4 January 2004.

Greenspan, A. (2003b), Prepared Statement, US Senate, Committee on Banking, Housing, and Urban Affairs, Hearing on the State of Financial Literacy and Education in American, 5 February.

Guiso, L. *et al.* (2000), "Household Portfolios: An International Comparison", *Working Paper*, No. 48, Cento Studi in Economia e Finanza (Center for Studies in Economics and Finance), Universita Degli Studi di Salerno, *www.dise.unisa.it/wo/wp48.pdf*, accessed 2 February 2005.

Lusardi, A. (2003), "Saving and the Effectiveness of Financial Education", *Working Paper*, No. 2003-14, Pension Research Council, The Wharton School, University of Pennsylvania, Philadelphia, *http://rider.wharton.upenn.edu/~prc/PRC/WP/WP2003-14.pdf*, accessed 11 January 2004.

OECD (2002), *OECD Economic Outlook*, No. 72, December, Annex Table 56, OECD, Paris.

United Nations (2003), *World Population Prospects: The 2002 Revision Population Database*, Population Division, United Nations, New York, *http://esa.un.org/unpp/p2k0data.asp*, accessed 2 February 2005.

van Ark, B. (2002), "Understanding Productivity and Income Differentials Among OECD Countries, A Survey", *Review of Economic Performance and Social Progress*, Vol. 2, Institute for Research on Public Policy, Montreal, *www.csls.ca/repsp/2/barvanark.pdf*, accessed 3 February 2005.

ISBN 92-64-01256-7
Improving Financial Literacy
Analysis of Issues and Policies
© OECD 2005

Chapter 3

Assessment of the Financial Literacy of Consumers

Financial literacy surveys can be used by policymakers to identify the financial skills and knowledge most lacking among consumers and to establish a baseline measurement of financial literacy with which to assess the effectiveness of financial literacy programmes. The existence of financial literacy surveys in half of the OECD countries – fifteen OECD countries have conducted or will conduct surveys – indicates that policymakers as well as financial institutions increasingly recognise the importance of benchmarking this knowledge among the population.[1]

The OECD identified surveys in twelve countries for which results are already available.[2] All of the surveys conclude that the financial literacy level of most consumers is very low. Among these surveys, the OECD selected six surveys in five countries (Australia, Japan, Korea, the United States and the United Kingdom) for which there is detailed information on methodology, results, questions asked, and target groups.[3] These six surveys exhibit two different approaches to measuring financial literacy. One approach is to give respondents an objective test that measures their knowledge and understanding of financial terms and their ability to apply financial concepts to particular situations. Surveys of this type were undertaken in the United States and Korea and were targeted to high school students. The other approach is to ask respondents for a self-assessment, or for their perceptions, of their financial understanding and knowledge, as well as for their attitudes toward financial instruments, decisions, information and its receipt. This is the approach used by the surveys undertaken in the United Kingdom, Japan, and Australia, although the Australian survey also includes some more objective measures of financial literacy. More detail on these surveys is provided in Annex A.

Key findings of financial literacy surveys[4]

Although the surveys differed in target audience, approach to measuring financial literacy, and survey methodology, there are a number of similarities in the results.

One result common to all the surveys is the low level of financial understanding among respondents

- Both Korean and American high school students had failing scores – that is, they answered fewer than 60 per cent of the questions correctly – on tests designed to measure students' ability to choose and manage a credit card, knowledge to save and invest for retirement, and awareness of risk and the importance of insuring against it. (Table A.1 in Annex A.)

- Neither ownership of stocks nor the receipt of a regular allowance increased the scores of American and Korean students on the tests of financial literacy. However, those students who discussed money issues with their parents had higher (although not passing) scores than students who did not. American students with a savings account and Korean students with a checking account had higher scores than students without such accounts.

- The Japanese Consumer Survey on Finance finds that 71 per cent of adult respondents had no knowledge about investment in equities and bonds, 57 per cent had no knowledge of financial products in general, and 29 per cent had no knowledge about insurance, pensions, and tax.

- The Australian survey (which surveyed adults) notes that 21 per cent of those who received and read their superannuation statement did not understand it. When asked to answer four questions about a sample bank statement, only 49 per cent of respondents could answer all four questions correctly.

The surveys that included questions about respondents' social characteristics find that financial understanding is correlated with education and income levels

- In Australia, the lowest levels of financial literacy are associated with low levels of education (year 10 or less), unemployment or low skilled work, low incomes (household income under $20 000), low levels of savings (under $5 000), being single, and being at either end of the age profile (18 to 24 year olds and those aged 70 years or older). (Table A.4 in Annex A.)

- In the United Kingdom, individuals in the lower social grades and the lowest income band, as well as young people aged 18 to 24, are likely to be the least receptive consumers – uninterested, unconfident, and least active. By contrast, the higher social grades, those with higher income, young couples and older respondents with no family are more likely to be sophisticated financial consumers, knowing how to get the information they need and understanding the advice they receive.

- In the Korean and American surveys, scores broken down by demographic characteristics indicate that students from families with less educated parents and/or students who have low income and professional expectations score the lowest.

Respondents often feel they know more about financial matters than is actually the case

- Respondents in the United States, the United Kingdom, and Australia felt confident in their knowledge of financial issues even though when given a test on basic finance it is clear they had only a limited understanding of these issues. If consumers do not realise they need information, they will not be in a position to seek it.

- The survey in the United States finds that 65 per cent of students said that they are somewhat sure or very sure of their ability to manage their own finances. However, the scores of these students were not much higher than those of their less confident peers. This suggests that students are unable to judge accurately how capable they are to manage their money. This unsupported confidence might result in reduced demand for money management courses.

- When asked for their perceptions, most respondents to the Australian survey stated that they are financially literate. However, when asked to apply their financial knowledge to solve a particular problem, they demonstrated a lack of financial understanding. Although 67 per cent of respondents indicated that they understand the concept of compound interest, only 28 per cent correctly answered a problem using this concept.

Consumers feel financial information is difficult to find and understand

- The Japanese Consumer Survey on Finance finds that respondents felt frustrated about the difficulty of finding easy-to-understand information on financial products. When asked about the financial information provided by various organisations and companies, 39 per cent of respondents said they had not seen much information and 29 per cent found the content of the information difficult and hard to follow.

- The British survey finds that consumers do not actively seek out financial information. The information they do receive is acquired by luck or chance or hazard, for example, by picking up a pamphlet at a bank or having a chance talk with a bank employee. The British survey also finds that consumers' perceived complexity of financial products is one reason given for not going ahead with purchase.

Implications for financial literacy surveys

- To enable better cross-country comparisons it would be useful to distribute a single questionnaire in member countries that asked similar types of questions. This questionnaire could consist of a core set of questions that would be asked in all countries plus a supplement containing questions that could vary by country. Such a questionnaire would facilitate comparisons of financial literacy across countries while still allowing flexibility for countries to ask about special, country-specific issues.

- Objective tests of financial concepts are a better way of measuring financial literacy than are surveys which ask respondents to provide a self-assessment of their understanding of financial issues. However, a comparison of consumers' self-assessments with their response to objective questions that test their financial understanding could indicate to policymakers where the largest discrepancies are between what consumers believe they know and what they actually know.

- Financial literacy surveys can be used to ask questions about the availability, clarity and delivery methods of financial information. If policymakers hope to improve the financial literacy level of consumers they must know the best way to reach these consumers (e.g. through television, brochures, Internet, etc.) and the most effective way to present this information.

- Looking at financial literacy scores by demographic characteristics helps policymakers determine which consumer groups are most in need of which type of financial education. Such knowledge of consumer needs will help policymakers to target the appropriate financial information to where it is most needed.

Lessons for financial education programmes

- Responses to the survey questions indicate that many consumers have little knowledge about common financial products and lack information on such basic financial issues as the relationship between risk and return. Thus, providers will need to focus on providing financial education programmes through a variety of channels to reach as many consumers as possible and on ensuring that this information is easy for consumers to understand. For example, policymakers might consider conducting national campaigns to raise awareness about the importance of understanding financial issues.

- Although financial literacy levels are low in general for consumers, they are especially low for certain groups of consumers, such as the less-educated, those at the lower end of the income distribution, and minorities. Thus, policymakers should consider targeting financial education programmes to those groups of consumers who are most in need of it. Policymakers will also need to decide the best way to convey this information to the target audience.

- The fact that consumers feel more confident than their actual financial knowledge warrants suggests that an important aspect of financial education programmes is increasing consumers' awareness of their need for financial information. If consumers are not aware they need financial information, they will not seek it out. Thus policymakers need to think about the best ways to reach these consumers and convince them that they need financial education.

- Consumers receive financial information through a variety of sources and these sources tend to differ according to demographic characteristics. Many consumers, notably those with lower incomes, receive financial information through television programmes. A large number of consumers prefer to receive financial information through personal contact, such as consumer help lines or personal advisors. Policymakers will need to think about the most effective delivery channel for the consumers they are targeting.

● Many consumers accept without question what their financial advisor recommends. Thus, providers of financial education programmes should make available information on the types of advisors, questions to ask of an advisor, and objective and disinterested information on the use of financial advisors.

● Many consumers believe that financial information is difficult to find and understand. This suggests that another important role for financial education programmes is to inform consumers about where to go to find information and to present this information in ways that are easy for consumers to understand.

More detailed information on the Assessment of the Financial literacy of Consumers can be found in Annex A.

Notes

1. Unless otherwise noted, the information about these surveys comes from responses to the OECD's questionnaire on financial education sent to delegates of the Committee on Financial Markets. Other sources are given in the references at the end of this chapter.

2. Surveys recently conducted or planned by three countries – Hungary, Ireland and Canada – are not discussed.

3. Surveys in three of the other seven countries target investors. The Capital Markets Board of Turkey sponsored a survey in May and June of 2003 that found that investors in many cases do not read and study the prospectus that is sent to them. A survey conducted in 2001 by the Hong Kong, China, Securities and Futures Commission found that two-thirds of respondents felt that their understanding of the basics of investing was insufficient. In Portugal, the Securities Market Commission conducted surveys of investors in 1998 and 2000, and used the results to develop its investor education programmes. The remaining surveys target consumers. In Italy, both the Bank of Italy and a private research centre have surveyed households about financial issues. In Austria, consumer behaviour surveys have been conducted by several universities in Vienna and have found that consumers frequently lack basic knowledge about current accounts, loans, and personal insurance. In Germany, a survey commissioned by Commerzbank AG in 2003 found that although 80 per cent of respondents felt confident about their understanding of financial issues, only 42 per cent were able to answer correctly just half of the 35 survey questions (German Embassy Online, 2003). In France, the Financial Markets Authority commissioned a survey on the economic and financial education of savers. Three-fourths of the respondents stated that they knew little about finance, one in two did not feel adequately prepared to choose a financial product, and two-thirds viewed investments as extremely complex (AMF, 2005).

4. Additional information on the results is provided in Annex A.

IMPROVING FINANCIAL LITERACY – ISBN 92-64-01256-7 – © OECD 2005

References

Autorité des Marchés financiers (AMF) (2005), *Pour l'Éducation Économique et Financière des Épargnants*, présentation du rapport du groupe de travail, *www.amf-france.org/documetns/general/6080_1.pdf*, accessed 30 June 2005.

ANZ Banking Group (2003), *ANZ Survey of Adult Financial Literacy in Australia*, *www.anz.com/aus/aboutanz/Community/Programs/FinLitResearch.asp*, accessed 21 October 2004.

Central Council for Financial Services Information (2002), *Public Opinion Survey on Household Financial Assets and Liabilities*, *www.saveinfo.or.jp/e*, accessed 21 June 2004.

Financial Services Authority (FSA) (2000), "Better Informed Consumers", *Consumer Research Document*, #1, *www.fsa.gov.uk/pubs/consumer-research/crpr01.pdf*, accessed 18 August 2003.

German Embassy Online (2003), "Survey Finds Germans Lack Investment Savvy", *The Week in Germany: Economics and Technology*, 6 June, *www.germany-info.org*, accessed 17 February 2004.

Mandell, L. (2001), *Improving Financial Literacy: What Schools and Parents Can and Cannot Do*, The Jump$tart Coalition for Personal Financial Literacy, Washington D.C., *www.jumpstart.org/pdf/financialliteracybook.pdf*, accessed 29 September 2003.

Mandell, L. (2004), 2004 Personal Finance Survey of High School Seniors, executive summary, The Jumpstart Coalition for Personal Financial Literacy, Washington D.C.,*www.jumpstart.org/download.cfm* , accessed 3 November 2004.

National Council on Economic Education (NCEE) (1999), *NCEE Standards in Economics: Survey of Students and the Public*, *www.ncee.net/cel/results.php*, accessed 3 november 2004.

ISBN 92-64-01256-7
Improving Financial Literacy
Analysis of Issues and Policies
© OECD 2005

Chapter 4

Investment/retirement Saving and Financial Education

Throughout the OECD countries, an increasing number of individuals are investing in financial products and services. One important contribution to this increase is the rise in the number of workers participating in defined contribution plans. And it is clear that many of these workers faced with the responsibility for investing their retirement contributions need help. According to a recent survey by John Hancock Financial Services, less than one-quarter of Americans of working age consider themselves to be "knowledgeable investors". Even among this group there is "considerable confusion" about financial matters (Francis, 2004). A survey by the Royal Bank of Canada finds that respondents consider choosing the right investments for a retirement savings plan to be more stressful than going to the dentist (Canadian Press, 2005). In the United Kingdom, the Financial Services Agency ranks as one of its main concerns the fact that consumers are making financial decisions based on inadequate understanding (Wheatcroft, 2004).

Of even more concern is the lack of awareness among consumers of the importance of saving for retirement. According to a recent survey by the Employee Benefit Research Institute, four out of ten American workers state that they are not putting any money aside for retirement (Helman and Paladino, 2004). A recent report in New Zealand concludes that many individuals in that country are either "unwilling or not able" to save enough for retirement, adding that about 30 per cent of households spend more than they earn (Weir, 2004). An additional concern is that those who are saving are not saving enough. The Bank of Ireland Life has expressed concern that many individuals investing for their retirement are not saving enough, adding that only about 52 per cent of workers aged 20 to 69 are investing in a pension (Business World, 2004).

This lack of awareness is especially worrisome as private pension plans and personal savings are likely to play an even more important role in retirement income in the future, with the result that individuals will need to be even more knowledgeable about saving for retirement. Employers are increasingly concerned about their employees' levels of saving. A recent survey by Hewitt Associates finds that only 18 per cent of large employers are confident their employees are saving enough for retirement. In addition to offering financial education programmes, many of these employers are now automatically enrolling employees in their 401(k) plans (Hewitt Associates, 2005). More generally, it could be recommended that employers be required to alert employees when they are aware that employees' contributions to their defined-contribution pension plan are significantly insufficient for adequate retirement income.

Financial education can provide workers with the information and skills to make wise investment choices for both their pension plans and any individual savings plans. By providing accurate, objective, and easily understandable information, such as a discussion of investment terms and descriptions of the features of different types of investment, and by equipping workers with the skills to absorb this information, financial education can help them select the investment products and services that are most appropriate for their individual situations. Financial education can also alert workers to be wary of schemes that promise high returns with low risks and help them ask the right questions about financial products and services. For example, a financially educated investor would know that he or she should not concentrate an entire investment portfolio in one stock, whether this is personal savings or an employer-provided defined contribution plan.

Financial education programmes can also help governments explain to the public the need for pension reform, typically the need to move in whole or in part from a traditional pay-as-you-go programme to a funded programme. The recent Slovak government media campaign is an example of a successful explanation of pension reform (Jurninová, 2004). In addition, in countries in which pension reform is occurring, it is very important that workers be aware of the necessity of making sound investment decisions and that they be provided with the information and skills that will enable them to do so. Financial education programmes can explain these pension reforms to consumers and help consumers make appropriate choices.

Current financial education programmes on saving and investing for retirement[1]

The OECD's survey of financial education programmes in member countries identified 16 countries that already provide, or are planning to provide, workers with information about pensions and how to invest their savings for retirement: Austria, Australia, Canada, Finland, Germany, Hungary, Italy, Japan, the Netherlands, New Zealand, Poland, Portugal, Turkey, Mexico, Sweden, the United Kingdom, and the United States. A more detailed description of selected programmes offered in these countries can be found in Annex B.

The most frequently used way of providing retirement savings information is through publications. These come in a variety of forms including brochures, magazines, booklets, guidance papers, newsletters, annual reports, direct mail documents, letters and disclosure documents. The majority of providers of these publications are from the public (or semi-public) sector: government agencies, ministries (of finance and social affairs), central banks, and regulatory and supervisory authorities. Consumers' and employees' associations as well as pension fund organisations are also important providers of these publications. Most publications are intended for a broad selection of investor population groups, but a few target specific groups including employees and members of specific pension funds.

The next most frequently used method of providing retirement savings information is through Web sites. The topics covered and providers of these Web sites are similar to those of publications. Most sites are intended for all investor population groups. An example of such a site is that of the Investor Education Fund in Canada, which contains several investment calculators and a variety of resources to help investors determine their risk level. In contrast, one initiative in Poland is targeted particularly to insurance and pension fund clients. Another project in Sweden is a Web portal grouping together the numerous information pages and Web sites already in existence which provide information and advice on the many different pension systems available to future Swedish retirees.

Training courses are also often used to deliver financial information on pensions. Providers range from employers (United States) to pension fund organisations (Netherlands) and an independent retirement investment information service (Australia). Courses also tend to be targeted at a specific population group – employees or company board members and/or policymakers, for example.

A number of countries have undertaken public education campaigns for the promotion of financial education on investment and saving. Providers of these campaigns span the public, semi-public, private and independent non-profit sectors and include regulatory and supervisory bodies, government agencies, and consumer associations. They also include a variety of methods of provision – brochures, Web sites, radio, television, etc.

Evaluations of financial education programmes with respect to investment/retirement

Given the increasing responsibility of individuals for their retirement incomes, it is important that they make the best choices possible. Improving the financial knowledge of individuals will certainly play a role. Therefore, an assessment of the effectiveness of financial education programmes in improving this knowledge and an evaluation of what approaches have worked well is important.

The evaluations of financial education programmes can be classified as either subjective or objective. The subjective evaluations ask participants in the financial education programme for their views about the information provided and about whether in response to this information they intend to change their behaviour by, for example, saving more or opening up a retirement account. This can be done by surveying participants both before and after they have taken a course in financial education. The objective evaluations identify some goal, such as an increase in participation rates or in contribution rates to a defined contribution plan, and then use data and statistical techniques to determine whether there is a significant relationship between attendance at a financial education programme and change in the goal variables.[2]

Subjective evaluations

Financial education seminars have an effect on individuals' retirement goals and savings behaviour according to one study. Clark, *et al.* (2001), look at responses to questionnaires distributed at 60 TIAA-CREF financial education seminars held at educational institutions and non-profit organisations between March 2001 and May 2002.[3] Participants completed a survey on retirement goals, attended a one-hour financial seminar, and then filled out a second questionnaire to see if these retirement goals had changed. In analysing the results, the authors find that 34 per cent of the participants changed either their retirement income goal or their retirement age goal in response to the seminar. Ninety-one per cent of respondents reported that they anticipated making changes to their retirement savings plans. The authors conclude that the provision of financial information has an important effect on saving for retirement.

As discussed in the following section, these results do support those of other studies that use objective evaluation methods. There are several limitations to this study, however. This survey looks at the responses of those who chose to attend the seminar and, who therefore, might be more disposed to change their behaviour than individuals not attending the seminar. In other words, their behaviour might not be representative of the average worker. More important, there was no follow-up to see if respondents actually carried out the actions they said they intended to do. There can be a big difference between what individuals plan to do and that they actually do.

Several studies have used subjective evaluations to look at how consumers prefer to receive information on financial issues. Rhine and Toussaint-Comeau (2002), using data from a household survey conducted in Chicago, find that socioeconomic, demographic, and life-style characteristics affect consumers' preferences as to receipt of financial information. They find, for example, that lower-income, less educated adults are less likely to select the Internet as means of finding information about personal finance issues, but are more likely to prefer formal courses offered in the local community. Low-income and minority consumers are also more likely to select radio programmes as a means of receiving information about financial issues. Older adults and minorities are more likely to choose seminars as their preferred means of receiving financial information.

Hilgert and Hogarth (2003) also ask consumers about preferred sources of information on financial topics. They find that more financially sophisticated consumers prefer the Internet. In general, however, households prefer to receive financial information through media sources such as television, radio, magazines and newspapers as well as through informational videos and brochures. Consequently, financial education will need to be disseminated through all available media in order to ensure a wide coverage and exposure.

Objective evaluations

A 1996 NBER study finds that participation in and contributions to voluntary savings plans [401(k) plans] are greater when employers offer frequent retirement seminars (Bayer et al., 1996).[4] The authors find that non-highly compensated workers experience the largest effects, with a 12 percentage point increase in participation rates and a one percentage point increase in the contribution rate.[5] Highly compensated workers experience an increase in participation of six percentage points but no increase in contribution rate. Lusardi (2003) also finds that attending a retirement seminar increases workers' savings. The effect of the seminars is especially strong for those with low levels of education and those with low levels of savings. Using data from the Health and Retirement Study, she finds that attending retirement seminars increases financial wealth by 18 per cent. For those at the bottom of the distribution, the increase in financial wealth is 70 per cent.

The evidence on the effectiveness of brochures and other written material is more mixed. Bayer et al. (1996), find that written materials, such as newsletters and summary plan descriptions, have no effect on participation and contribution rates. However, Clark and Schieber (1998), using employment records gathered by Watson Wyatt Worldwide from 19 firms covering 40 000 employees, find that certain types of written material do have an effect. They compare three levels of plan communications: distribution of plan enrolment forms and required periodic statements of account balances, provision of generic newsletters related to participation in 401(k) plans, and provision of materials specifically tailored to the 401(k) plan sponsored by the individual company. The authors find that the provision of generic newsletters increases participation by 15 percentage points while the provision of information specific to the individual company's 401(k) plan increases participation an additional 21 percentage points. Thus, employee participation in voluntary retirement plans can be increased by 36 percentage points if a company provides both generic and specifically tailored financial information. The authors also find that the provision of information specific to the company's 401(k) plan increases the contribution rate by two percentage points. However, the contribution rate is not significantly affected by the provision of generic newsletters on 401(k) plans.

A survey by Ernst and Young (2004) of human resources and employee benefits professionals in a cross section of large employers finds that personalised counselling programmes are most important in changing participant behaviour and that financial information alone is not sufficient. In most of the firms surveyed there is little response to traditionally provided financial education such as brochures upon enrolment and quarterly statements thereafter. When employers use more personalised programmes such as telephone or in-person counselling, there is a substantial increase in the percentage change in participant investing. The study concludes that one-on-one counselling is better able to help employees understand the importance of saving and to equip them to determine the best course of action to meet their financial needs. However, such counselling can be expensive for employers to provide.

Effect of individual behaviour on financial decisions

Improved financial education is the appropriate response if lack of financial information or skills is the reason for low levels of saving. However, financial education is only one factor influencing financial behaviour. There have been an increasing number of studies in behavioural economics that relate financial and savings behaviour to psychological factors. For example, several studies find that while a certain percentage of consumers are dedicated savers who think that individuals should take responsibility for their retirement, a much larger percentage have a "live for today" attitude and prefer to spend money than to save it. Other studies find that many households would like to save more but lack the willpower or are overwhelmed by too much choice. The findings of these studies and the existence of heterogeneous savings behaviour across consumers might have important implications for the design and implementation of effective financial education programmes.[6]

MacFarland, et al. (2003), study the link between psychological attitudes towards money and retirement planning using the results of a survey of 1 141 randomly selected individuals in Vanguard recordkeeping plans. The authors find that attitudes are important and are linked to specific behavioural differences with respect to plan participation, investment decisions, and engagement with retirement plan accounts. They find in their sample that slightly more than 50 per cent of participants have no strong retirement goals and lack the discipline to set and adhere to goals; consider financial matters to be a source of stress, anxiety, and confusion; or are uninterested in the future.

For individuals such as these, retirement plans that rely on the voluntary decisions of participants will have only a limited ability to assure retirement security. Thus, the existence of heterogeneous savings behaviour across consumers implies that different subgroups of consumers/investors will require different financial education programmes.

These findings suggest that in order to meet the needs of those consumers who are "non-planners", financial education programmes will need to emphasise simpler decisions, less information, reduced complexity, and fewer choices. The financial education programmes must emphasise tangible present-day (as opposed to some future day) benefits and must be explicit and direct. In fact, the authors conclude that, based on their findings, for some consumers in this group of non-planners, financial education may not be the only solution. What might be best for this group is automatic enrolment in a 401(k) plan with the appropriate defaults with respect to contribution rates and investment allocation so that even if they do nothing they will approach an adequate level of savings for retirement.

Choi et al. (2002), study the impact of automatic enrolment in 401(k) plans using both a survey of individual savings adequacy and an analysis of administrative data on the 401(k) savings behaviour of employees in several large corporations that had implemented changes in their defined contribution plans.[7] The authors note that sponsors of financial education programmes need to keep in mind a key behaviour variable – that employees often follow the "path of least resistance". In other words, employees will often do what is easiest, which may be nothing, a phenomenon that the authors call a "passive decision". Thus, by changing the design of the 401(k) plans so that the default is automatic enrolment when the employee becomes eligible, participation rates can be greatly increased and few employees ever take action to disenroll. Participation rates under automatic enrolment are between 86 and 96 per cent after six months of tenure at the companies studied. Before automatic enrolment, participation rates at six months of tenure were between 26 and 43 per cent. The authors conclude that plan design can significantly affect the savings behaviour of individuals. Because few employees opt out of default options, employers' choices of default savings rates and default investment funds have significant effects on savings levels of employees.

Thaler and Benartzi (2001) address the issue of low savings rates in 401(k) plans and suggest an approach for increasing those rates. They base their approach on research showing that individuals prefer future opportunities to save over current ones, that due to inertia and procrastination individuals tend to stay in a programme once enrolled, and that due to loss aversion individuals are reluctant to increase their retirement savings if this means a reduction in take-home pay. This research on individuals' behaviour was used to design the Save More Tomorrow (SMT) programme, which gives workers the option to commit themselves now to increase their savings rate later, for example, each time they get a raise. This programme has been introduced in several firms. Where it was used in conjunction with an investment consultant who met with the employees and discussed savings options, the workers who joined the SMT plan tripled their saving rates in 28 months from 3.5 per cent to 11.6 per cent.

Research also shows that the number of funds offered by a 401(k) plan has an effect on participation. Recent research on consumer choice has found that too many options lead to "choice overload" with the result that consumers are less motivated to choose and less motivated to commit to that choice (Iyengar *et al.*, 2003). Too many options increase the likelihood of not choosing optimally and thus increase the burden on consumers. This burden is likely to be even higher if there are costs associated with making a non-optimal choice or if consumers would need to commit significant time and effort in order to make informed comparisons among available options. This research finds that participation rates peak when only two funds are offered. As the number of funds increases, participation rates decline. Each time the number of funds is increased by ten there is a corresponding decrease of 1.5 to 2 per cent in the participation rate. One implication arising from this research is that pension plan providers should consider using a "tiered" approach in which a limited number of options, say fewer than ten, is offered on the first tier. However, one of the options in this tier would be "additional funds", the choice of which would provide sophisticated workers with many more options. This way those individuals who cannot handle numerous options would not be overwhelmed while those who want more choices would be able to have them. Regardless of the number of options available to workers, financial education is needed to help workers learn about their options and make appropriate choices.

Conclusions and implications for design and implementation of financial education programmes

- Employer-provided financial education seminars and personalised financial counselling programmes increase worker participation in and contributions to voluntary savings plans [401(k) plans]. The impact of brochures and other written material is not so obvious with the available research disagreeing on whether there is an effect on consumer financial behaviour.

- For plan providers dealing simultaneously with workers who have very little knowledge and need simple explanations and with workers who are quite sophisticated and want detailed information, one solution is the use of a "tiered" approach. In such an approach, the simplest explanations and most limited number of choices are offered in the lowest tier. However, one of the choices at this level is "more funds" or "more information" so that more sophisticated workers can have access to additional options.

- In general, households prefer to receive financial information about retirement through media sources such as TV, radio, magazines and newspapers as well as through informational videos and brochures. However, socioeconomic, demographic and life-style characteristics affect these preferences.

- To overcome such psychological behaviours as procrastination and inertia, it might be necessary to complement financial education programmes with automatic enrolment in defined contribution plans accompanied by default contribution rates and default investment allocations.

- There is no such thing as a one-size-fits-all financial education programme that will address the needs of all workers. Employers and plan providers will have to be flexible in the provision of financial education programmes and offer a variety of approaches.

More detailed information on the Investment/Retirement Saving and Financial Education can be found in Annex B.

Notes

1. Information in this section comes from responses to the OECD's questionnaire on financial education sent to delegates of the Committee on Financial Markets.

2. With respect to 401(k) plans, there are five behaviours that can be monitored to measure the impact of financial education: changes in participation rates, changes in contribution rates, changes in investment allocations, loan activity, and rollovers by terminated employees.

3. TIAA-CREF are non-profit organisations providing financial products to individuals in education, research, and health care. Topics discussed at these seminars include the amount of retirement income needed to maintain pre-retirement consumption, the amount of saving needed to achieve the retirement income goal, and the risk-return characteristics of alternative investments. Participants were also asked if they intend to change the allocation of their invested funds in response to the seminar. The sample consists of 663 participants who completed both questionnaires.

4. The authors used data from the 1993 and 1994 versions of the KPMG Peat Marwick Retirement Benefits Survey. This survey included approximately 1 100 employers selected at random from a list of al private and public employers in the United States with at least 200 employees. Employers were asked about the administration, features and employee utilisation of their retirement plans, as well as the extent to which they provided financial education and guidance to their employees.

IMPROVING FINANCIAL LITERACY – ISBN 92-64-01256-7 – © OECD 2005

5. Given that the average contribution rate is three per cent, an increase of one percentage point represents an increase of 33 per cent in the contribution rate.

6. These findings also suggest that, in some cases, a strengthening of consumer protection and of the regulation of financial institutions might be required to address deficiencies in financial capacity.

7. By matching responses to their survey with administrative data, the authors determine that almost none of the employees who reported that they intended to increase their savings rate in the next two months actually did so.

References

Bayer, P., D. Bernheim and K. Scholz (1996), "The Effects of Financial Education in the Workplace: Evidence from a Survey of Employers", *Working Paper*, No. 5655, National Bureau of Economic Research.

Business World (2004), "BoI Warns-1 M Hve No Pension Plan", 27 September.

Canadian Press (2005), "Retirement Saving, Financial Planning More Stressful Than Seeing the Dentist", 21 February.

Choi, J. *et al.* (2002), "Defined Contribution Plans: Plan Rules, Participant Decisions, and the Path of Least Resistance", *Working Paper*, 2002-3, Pension Research Council, The Wharton School, University of Pennsylvania, Philadelphia, *http:// rider.wharton.upenn.edu/~prc/PRC/WP/WP2002-3.pdf*, accessed 11 January 2004.

Clark, R. *et al.* (2003), "Financial Education and Retirement Savings", paper presented at the conference on Sustainable Community Development: What Works, What Doesn't, and Why, sponsored by the Federal Reserve System, Washington D.C., 27-28 March, *www.chicagofed.org/cedric/seeds_of_growth_2003_conference_session1.cfm*.

Clark, R. and S. Schieber (1998), "Factors Affecting Participation Rates and Contribution Levels in 401(k) Plans", in O. Mitchell and S. Schieber (eds.), *Living with Defined Contribution Plans*. University of Pennsylvania Press, Philadelphia.

Ernst and Young LLP Human Capital Practice (2004), *The Role That Financial Education Programs Play in Influencing Participant Behavior in 401(k) Plans*, *www.ey.com/global/ download.nsf/US/Financial_Education_Programs_in_401k_Plans/$file/ Fin_Ed_401k_plans.pdf*, accessed 2 March 2004.

Francis, D. (2004), "Ownership Society: Why the US Can't Buy In", *The Christian Science Monitor*, 27 September.

Helman, R. and V. Paladino (2004), "Will Americans Ever Become Savers? The 14th Retirement Confidence Survey, 2004", EBRI, *Issue Brief*, No. 268, Employee Benefit Research Institute (EBRI), Washington D.C.

Hewitt Associates (2005), "Hewitt Survey Reveals New Employer Trends in Retirement", *Press Release*, 18 January, *http://was4.hewitt.com/hewitt/resource/newsroom/pressrel/ 2005/01-18-05.pdf*.

Hilgert, M. and J. Hogarth (2003), "Household Financial Management: The Connection Between Knowledge and Behavior", *Federal Reserve Bulletin*, Washington D.C., *www.federalreserve.gov/Pubs/Bulletin/2003/03index.htm*, accessed 25 September 2003.

Iyengar, S., W. Jiang and G. Huberman (2003), "How Much Choice is Too Much?: Contributions to 401(k) Retirement Plans", *Working Paper*, 2003-10, Pension Research Council, The Wharton School, University of Pennsylvania, Philadelphia, *http:// rider.wharton.upenn.edu/~prc/PRC/WP/WP2003-10.pdf*, accessed 29 November 2004.

Jurninová, M. (2004), "Pension Media Blitz Targets Public", *The Slovak Spectator*, October 11.

Lusardi, A. (2003), "Saving and the Effectiveness of Financial Education", *Working Paper*, 2003-14, Pension Research Council, The Wharton School, University of Pennsylvania, Philadelphia, *http://rider.wharton.upenn.edu/~prc/PRC/WP/WP2003-14.pdf*, accessed 11 January 2004.

MacFarland, D., C. Marconi and S. Utkus (2003), "Money Attitudes and Retirement Plan Design: One Size Does Not Fit All", *Working Paper*, 2003-11, Pension Research Council, The Wharton School, University of Pennsylvania, Philadelphia, *http://rider.wharton.upenn.edu/~prc/PRC/WP/WP2003-11.pdf*, accessed 25 March 2004.

Rhine, S. and M. Toussaint-Comeau (2002), "Consumer Preferences in the Delivery of Financial Information: A Summary", *Consumer Interests Annual*, Vol. 48, *www.consumerinterests.org/files/public/FinancialInformation-02.pdf*, accessed 30 July 2003.

Thaler, R. and S. Benartzi (2001), "Save More Tomorrow: Using Behavioural Economics to Increase Employee Saving", *Working Paper*, Graduate School of Business, University of Chicago, Chicago, *http://gsbwww.uchicago.edu/fac/richard.thaler/research/SMarT14.pdf*, accessed 28 June 2004.

Wheatcroft, P. (2004), "'Lender, beware' is FSA's Advice", *The Times*, 21 January.

Weir, J. (2004), "The Push to Save for Retirement", *Fairfax New Zealand Limited*, August 31.

ISBN 92-64-01256-7
Improving Financial Literacy
Analysis of Issues and Policies
© OECD 2005

Chapter 5

Financial Education on Credit and Debt

In recent years across OECD countries, governments, financial institutions and others concerned about social welfare have become increasingly worried about the growing levels of debt taken on by consumers. Increased mortgage borrowing, the misuse of credit cards and predatory lending have resulted in excess indebtedness,[1] a rise in credit delinquencies, insolvencies and personal bankruptcies. Yet the abilities of consumers to use credit effectively and manage their money successfully are fundamental life skills. Failure to develop debt management skills can cause consumers to suffer, at best, financial distress and, at worst, major crises, which can have severe consequences and lead to significant losses for financial institutions (as creditors). Despite this risk, the essential financial knowledge and skills needed to manage personal credit and prevent excess-indebtedness or repair bad credit are not generally provided in secondary or tertiary education, as neither of these subjects (nor any other modules related to financial education) are yet part of the regular curriculum in OECD countries. Thus, most students graduate from schools and universities without proper financial knowledge and without skills to manage credit and debt. Focusing on five countries – Austria, Canada, Korea, the United Kingdom and the United States- this chapter presents the two main components of household credit and debt (mortgage/housing and consumer credit), discusses recent trends in the area, the main causes and consequences of the problem, and the importance of financial education in contributing to a solution.[2] It then gives an overview of existing preventive and curative credit education programmes, discusses findings of selected programme evaluations and the main policy implications for programme design.[3]

The importance of resolving over-indebtedness and the benefits of financial education[4]

Household debt consists of two main types of credit: a) (non-mortgage) consumer credit; and b) mortgage credit. The past two decades have witnessed a rise in this household debt as a share of disposable income in several OECD countries.[5] For the United Kingdom and the United States, data show an increase in household liabilities outstanding at the end of the period 1995-2003, as well as a significant rise in household debt as a share of personal disposable income from 1992 to 2003 (OECD, 2004b). In the United Kingdom and the United States, mortgage debt rose as a percentage of total household liabilities from 1995 to 2003 (OECD, 2004b). Meanwhile, growth in non-mortgage related debt (hereafter consumer credit) has also exceeded that of income over the past decade, but remains a smaller component of total household debt than mortgage debt (Debelle, 2004). Consumer credit as a percentage of disposable income increased just slightly from 1995-2003 in Austria, the United Kingdom and the United States (OECD, 2004b). In Korea, credit card debt has grown particularly rapidly in recent years (OECD, 2004a), and in Austria, household debt (a large share of which was foreign currency loans) rose from 2000 to 2003 (OECD, 2000). According to many observers, the increase in mortgage credit owes to three factors: low interest rates, rising house prices, and deregulation in the mortgage market (Debelle, 2004; Hamilton, 2003). Meanwhile, with respect to the upward trend in consumer borrowing, rising credit card debt has constituted the main source (Durkin, 2000). The past three decades has seen a considerable rise in the ownership and use of general-purpose credit cards with a revolving feature along with outstanding balances. Other factors contributing to the rise in debt across OECD countries include rapid developments in financial markets, products, and services (including consumer and mortgage loans) over the past few decades, which have increased the credit choices available to consumers but often rendered the choice and the nature of products far more complex (Braunstein and Welch, 2002; Greenspan, 2003; Boorstin, 2004). There has also been a major increase in the number of credit product providers (banks and Alternative Financial Services (AFS), for example) now offering similar types of credit products, and it is the rise in these AFS providers offering credit products that is probably the most worrying trend (CAB, 2001).

Accompanying these trends has been a rise in over-indebtedness (used to describe a situation when debt or debt service payments relative to income become a major burden for the borrower)[6] and its more serious consequences, namely personal delinquencies and bankruptcies, particularly in the United States (Marcuss, 2004). Certain population groups are more likely to be affected by debt and over-indebtedness than others. These are mainly younger individuals, who are especially prone to credit card misuse and those already in financial distress, who tend to have low incomes, bad credit histories and/or a lack of basic financial knowledge and skills. Consumers in financial distress are also easy targets for predatory lenders and subprime lenders, who often aggressively target low-income neighbourhoods with offers of easy credit. Such lending can place excess burdens on the disadvantaged, causing them to become entangled in a vicious cycle of borrowing at exorbitant interest rates and often tipping them over the edge into excess indebtedness.[7] Other groups (particularly in the United States) likely to have debt problems and desiring credit management as a priority topic in financial education programmes are employees and credit counselling clients. More than 2.5 million families and individuals are estimated to seek professional help with credit counselling each year, suggesting a great need for this service (Bailey et al., 2002).

As to why people experience excess indebtedness (or over-indebtedness), research finds a number of "inter-related personal reasons" to be the origin (UKDTI and UKDWP, 2004). Surveys conducted on the causes of over-indebtedness indicate that some of the reasons are a sudden change in personal circumstances such as job loss, relationship breakdown or illness which inevitably reduce income (Jentzsch, 2003). It is clear that, following any reduction in income, households with previously reasonable debt levels might not be able to pay their debts and thus experience excess indebtedness. Beyond these income reduction factors, however, it should be noted that over-commitment to various types of credit products is also highlighted in surveys (Jentzsch, 2003) as an important cause of over-indebtedness, and that this is in some cases related to personal finance mismanagement and financial illiteracy or a lack of the skills necessary to manage money well[8] (UKDTI and UKDWP, 2004). These results indicate that some effective ways of tackling over-indebtedness would be to improve personal finance management skills and enhance knowledge about credit options making it clear to an individual what his limits of credit use should be according to his own personal circumstances. Financial education initiatives can fulfil this role.

Household over-indebtedness can have major negative consequences on individuals, businesses, financial institutions and economies. For individuals, credit problems and delinquency can lead to an extra strain on relationships as couples struggle to save enough to pay off their continuing debt. This financial stress in turn can lead to illness, unemployment, divorce, and other harmful social consequences (such as break-up of the family unit), thus resulting in a vicious circle that further undermines the household's ability to break the debt cycle. With respect to individuals in businesses, stress accompanying debt problems could result in increased absenteeism and a loss of organisational commitment thus reducing productivity (Jinhee and Garman 2003, cited Mavrinac and Ping 2004). With delinquency or personal bankruptcy handling and management procedures proving costly for financial institutions, household over-indebtedness could cause some institutions to experience major financial losses thus negatively affecting their soundness as creditors (UKDTI and UKDWP, 2004). Finally, over-indebtedness can also have a negative impact on the economy via its effect on consumption expenditure in the long term: it can limit the levels of consumption expenditure and savings rates possible in the economy in the long-term (Ogawa and Wan, 2004; Murphy, 1999). Over-indebtedness can thus lead to a greater burden on public retirement programmes, with indebted workers unable to save as much for their retirement or participate fully in retirement plan contributions. Also, even if indebted individuals do manage to switch to individual accounts for funding, it stands to reason that the greater they are in debt, the less funds they will be able to invest in these accounts.

Credit education can benefit consumers and financial institutions in the following ways:

- There is evidence that, for a majority, debt problems are caused more by a lack of basic financial education and literacy than by a lack of income (Mavrinac and Ping, 2004). Consumers are not fully informed about credit products when they increasingly need to be. Identifying, evaluating, and comparing the increasingly vast selection of information available on different loan possibilities, making the best choice among a varied and complex array of credit instruments and identifying predatory lending necessitate, at the very least, a minimum level of financial literacy and skills to distinguish between products, and, preferably, a thorough knowledge and comprehension of the different instruments available. As evidence for this, one study shows that consumers with a better understanding of credit terms are, in general, able to significantly reduce their annual interest rate charges (Jinkook and Hogarth, 1999, cited Mavrinac and Ping, 2004).

- Credit education would benefit those groups most affected by debt. With greater financial literacy and credit knowledge, young people can understand how to better manage their credit card accounts, and employees can learn how to reduce their debt so that they can invest more in savings and retirement plans. Increased knowledge about finances and debt can also act as a safety net to protect the most vulnerable borrowers against fraud and abuse.

- With financially literate consumers more likely to avoid credit delinquency and personal bankruptcy filings, than those without financial knowledge and skills, financial institutions would benefit from an eventual reduction in their annual delinquency and personal bankruptcy-related losses.

Key findings on financial education programmes on credit and debt[9]

In the five selected countries, the OECD's research identifies approximately 72 financial education programmes[10] focusing on credit and debt topics, and with a preventive or curative approach.[11] The extent of the development of these programmes varies across the countries, with a considerable number of initiatives in the United Kingdom and the United States over the past decade, and a lesser number initiated more recently in Canada, Austria and Korea. The vast majority of these initiatives cover topics or issues related to consumer and personal credit (as opposed to mortgage debt), and most use a preventive approach.

Below is an overview of the main characteristics of these programmes. In accordance with the components of household debt mentioned earlier in the chapter, credit and debt education programmes have been broadly divided into three categories: 1) those dealing with consumer credit (such as credit card use, foreign currency loans, payday loans, home equity loans, consumer instalment loans, and other types of consumer credit – *e.g.* loans to buy cars and other durables); 2) those focused on mortgage/housing debt (which includes borrowing either for owner-occupation or for investment purposes) and related issues such as predatory lending; and 3) initiatives covering both of these categories.

Overview/typology of programmes

With respect to content and aims, the vast majority of initiatives cover topics or issues related to consumer and personal credit.[12] Of these, most offer preventive credit education. By far the majority of these preventive programmes on consumer credit cover two or more general topics related to credit and loans, including the importance of maintaining good credit, information on credit reports and credit scoring, the responsible use of credit cards, explaining identity theft, advice for controlling debt, and general credit and budget management skills. The ultimate aim of all these preventive programmes is to increase borrower protection against over-indebtedness. A few (mainly in the United States) focus only on the provision and sensible use of credit cards or the hazards of payday loans or home equity loans, and one initiative (in Austria) deals uniquely with the risks run by consumers when taking out foreign currency loans. Finally just over a third of all consumer credit programmes have both preventive and curative objectives and generally cover a broad range of the above-mentioned topic areas, with a few also giving advice to help consumers avoid scams or providing a credit counsellor locating service, for example.

Few of the credit and debt education programmes reviewed deal with issues and topics related to mortgage/housing loans, and all of those identified are based in the United States and the United Kingdom (perhaps unsurprising because, of all four countries, these two are the pioneers of the drive towards homeownership). Those with a preventive approach give tips for shopping around and finding the best mortgage deal possible, as well as warnings about how to avoid typical borrowing pitfalls, including watching out for predatory lenders. No mortgage debt education programmes with uniquely curative aims have been identified, but a few with combined preventive and curative approaches have been found. Almost all of these are based in the United Kingdom (with just one in the United States), and they provide more focused guidance on repayment methods, as well as information on arrears, repossession, and mortgage complaints along with information on the United Kingdom Mortgage Code. The United States-based programme was a post-purchase foreclosure prevention programme offering both counselling and financial assistance. Finally, a very small number of programmes apply to both credit types (most of these initiatives are curative), or cover credit and debt as just one financial topic among others.

The most frequently used delivery methods for the programmes are publications (including brochures, online/printed guides, public statements, action plans, briefing notes) and advisory services (including telephone helplines). Next come Internet offerings[13] (Web sites, Web portals and other online services); two or more delivery channels,[14] public educational campaigns and events (including presentations, lectures, conferences, symposia); training courses and seminars and other types of channels (such as CD ROMs and videos etc.) As with programmes for the unbanked and underserved, several credit education programmes identified are offered both in the national language of the country (e.g. English) and in the target population's native language (e.g. Spanish), either through bilingual instructors and/or the availability of interpreters and/or translated written materials.

With respect to providers, the largest number are non-profit organisations[15] and national government agencies.[16] Nonprofit organisations generally have well-developed training methods and extensive client networks, and their programmes are often financially supported by financial institutions, government, or both. Where governments are actively involved in credit education initiatives, their participation tends to be part of a public policy drive towards better consumer borrower protection. Other major suppliers of credit education programmes are central banks and financial institutions/service providers. Financial institutions supply programmes, for example, via their employees who act as professional educators and/or expert knowledge providers in credit training courses, seminars or in lectures. The OECD has also found limited provision from regulatory and supervisory authorities; consumer protection/professional organisations[17] (each of these three types offered an equal number of credit education programmes); and private sector companies; as well as a few programmes that are provided by a partnership of two providers and a few for which no details regarding provider are given.

Finally, as concerns the target population, the vast majority of programmes are intended for all credit consumers, including existing and prospective borrowers. Some other initiatives target debtors in financial difficulty, including mortgage holders who have been repossessed, and still others are intended (in order of preference) for homeowners (current and prospective) and first-time homebuyers, young people[18] – with Korea offering a significant selection of programmes to this group – and credit card users. The OECD has also found a few programmes targeted specifically to women, armed forces members and providers of/advisors in debt programmes, as well as one programme intended for parents of adolescents likely to be susceptible to misuse of credit.

Key findings for evaluations of credit education programmes[19]

Financial education programmes on mortgage and consumer credit, as opposed to regulation or government welfare assistance programmes in this area, aim to lower mortgage delinquency rates and consumer loan indebtedness levels as well as to protect borrowers from exploitation, not only in the short-term but also in the long-term. They can accomplish this through the provision of instruction, information and objective advice that will build the budget management tools necessary for borrowers to effectively manage their debts, and the financial understanding necessary for them to avoid the pitfalls that can so easily lead to over-indebtedness, thus increasing their future financial self-sufficiency. These programmes thus aim to have a mainly preventive role in the area of excess indebtedness, helping borrowers to acquire the financial tools and skills essential to managing their debts better on their own, prior to delinquency or bankruptcy and thus avoiding the need to resort to state assistance, for example, once the crisis caused by debt mismanagement has already taken place. However, it should be noted that most financial education on credit and debt can only contribute to resolving over-indebtedness and not provide a complete solution to the issues. Evaluations provide an indication of the effectiveness of credit programmes in meeting these aims.

The OECD identified only four evaluations of credit education programmes, which were mostly counselling initiatives and all were conducted in the United States. The evaluations offer some indications for what works and what does not in credit education. Although they highlight the best and most cost-effective delivery methods for financial training on mortgage and/or consumer debt management, the variety of methods studied are limited (mainly counselling), and there is clearly a need for other countries to conduct studies. The main findings of these evaluations and the implications to be drawn from them can be summarised as follows:

Findings applicable to mortgage and consumer credit education

Some borrowers are overwhelmed by the vast amounts of information available on loan products and often find this information overly complicated. For these individuals credit education needs to provide simpler information, first about the basics of credit management and financial skills and only after these fundamentals have been learnt, about more complex credit products. One problem is that programme providers are often targeting both individuals who have very little knowledge and need simple explanations along with individuals who are quite sophisticated and require more complex information.

One study finds that younger participants are more likely than those aged 55 and older to want to learn about consumer credit and debt management, suggesting a need for post-school adult consumer credit education, as well as credit education offered in schools, at least up until retirement age (O'Neill, 2000).

Mortgage education

- A study of a pre-purchase home ownership programme, Freddie Mac's Affordable Gold, finds that counselling can be of use in lowering mortgage delinquency rates (Hirad and Zorn, 2001). They find the type of counselling format to be the most important feature: one-on-one counselling sessions and to a lesser extent classroom and home study counselling are found to be the most valuable types of counselling formats. However, because these types of counselling are expensive to provide, it is implied that it would be best, from a cost-effectiveness point of view, to provide them only for the highest risk borrowers, and that, for lower risk borrowers other less costly counselling types (telephone counselling, for example) could suffice.

- According to a study of a post-purchase homeownership course, counselling combined with financial assistance is found to be more effective for high-risk borrower households than counselling alone.[20] In order to effectively establish the impact of counselling on mortgage repayment rates and debt outcomes both in the short- and long-term, it is suggested that follow-up studies of post-purchase homeownership courses should include control groups for comparison and track outcomes for households who took part in the study over a long period of time (Mallach [no date]). Follow-up studies involving these two elements are also recommendable for all mortgage debt education programmes.

Consumer credit education

- In a consumer credit education programme, where funding and resources allow, one-on-one counselling is also found to be an effective delivery method, having a positive impact on consumer credit use and payment behaviour even over an extended period (Elliehausen et al., 2002).

- Setting objectives and personal goals, such as reduction of debt below a particular level and one which is realistic for a consumer's circumstances, appears to be another successful programme feature (O'Neill et al., 2000). Participants in the Money 2000 programme expressed positive remarks about the structure, motivation, and accountability provided by the setting of concrete goals applicable to their personal lives.

- As with delivery to the unbanked and underserved population, the evaluations find personal contact during programmes to be an important feature (O'Neill, 2000). However, written class support materials (worksheets, checklists, self-assessment activities) are also considered appropriate, as is the flexibility for class content and information to be shared via other delivery materials (such as newsletters) for those who cannot attend class.

Summary of policy implications for financial education programmes on credit and debt

- With some adult consumers overwhelmed by too much information about credit products and finding this information to be overly complex, programme designers could consider dividing courses into two streams. One stream would be intended for less experienced borrowers lacking the basics of budget management (who should be encouraged and helped to continue to improve their general financial literacy and budget management skills) and the other for those who understand the credit market better (who could be given more complex information about credit products so that they can choose and transfer between products and understand the full implications of their use).

- Above all, with consumers often lacking the confidence necessary for challenging the shrewd marketing techniques used by credit salesmen, credit education programmes must build confidence in all consumers (no matter their ability range). More financially confident customers would be better able to challenge financial intermediaries selling them credit contracts, and take better charge of their debts in general.

- In order for consumers to learn most effectively, the real impact (in both the short- and long-term) and implications of debt problems on their everyday lives should be made clear – credit education should be taught at a level as personal as possible. According to one report, the best way for credit education to work is to simplify economic and financial concepts, which can be quite theoretical and complex (Hopley, 2003). Efforts should be made to apply them to "real life situations" and to link them to meaningful and applicable personal life goals outside of class.

- Some studies suggest that financial instruction on debt use should be incorporated into regular school curricula (US Treasury, 2002). However, others highlight the need for post-school adult credit education, too, at least up until retirement age.

The literature and evaluations reviewed in this chapter offer some indications for the best and most cost-effective delivery methods for financial education programmes covering mortgage credit and consumer debt. Financial education programmes for mortgage and consumer credit, as opposed to regulation or government welfare assistance programmes in this area, aim to lower mortgage delinquency rates and consumer loan indebtedness levels, as well as to protect borrowers from exploitation not only in the short term but also in the long term. The provision of instruction, information and objective advice will help consumers build the budget management tools necessary to effectively manage their debts, and the financial understanding necessary for them to avoid the pitfalls that can so easily lead to over-indebtedness. As a result, borrowers should become more self-sufficient in the future. Financial education programmes aim to have a mainly preventive role in the area of excess indebtedness, helping borrowers to acquire the financial tools and skills essential to managing their debts better on their own, which lessens the risks that they will become delinquent or be forced to declare bankruptcy. In so doing, financial education programmes help avoid the need for borrowers to resort to state assistance, for example, once the crisis caused by debt mismanagement has already begun. It should be noted, however, that most financial education programmes on credit and debt can only help to resolve over-indebtedness and do not provide a complete solution to the issues.

More detailed information on Financial Education on Credit and Debt can be found in Annex C.

Notes

1. Indebtedness can be measured as a ratio of debt to income. Two types of measures constructed by the US Federal Reserve Board, for example, are the household Debt Service Ratio (DSR), an estimate of debt payments to disposable personal income, and the Financial Obligations Ratio (FOR), which adds to the household Debt Service Ratio automobile lease payments, rental payments on tenant-occupied property, homeowners' insurance, and property tax payments.

2. Although rising debt levels and excess indebtedness have affected households in all OECD countries over the past decade, in their responses to the OECD's surveys on financial education, Austria, Canada, Korea and the United States stressed that their efforts in the financial education sphere would include the provision of credit and debt education programmes and the United Kingdom highlighted the role played by its government in providing credit information and by its voluntary sector in debt advice provision.

3. It should be noted that this chapter focuses mainly on adult, non-school credit and debt education programmes, but considering the importance of credit management among young people, a few programmes targeted to school/university students (though not part of any institutionalised curriculum) are also included.

4. For more details related to this section, see Annex C.

5. Figure C.1 in Annex C.

6. See the definition of over-indebtedness in DTI and DWP, 2004, *Tackling Over-Indebtedness Action Plan 2004*.

7. Predatory lending and sub-prime lending are thus aggravating factors of household over-indebtedness.

8. Results of a Survey on Reasons for Bankruptcy and Overindebtedness as summarised by Nicola Jentzsch.

9. For more details related to this section, see Annex C.

10. This number is by no means exhaustive.

11. Unless otherwise indicated, information on financial education programmes on credit and debt comes from responses of the CMF delegates to the OECD's questionnaire on financial education.

12. When considering content, it is important to note that several of the programmes identified covered a range of general financial education topics of which credit and debt was often just one component, or a component that had been added recently to programmes.

13. Care was taken to select only those Web sites/online services offering objective and unbiased information and advice. The OECD found during its research, that although not always obvious, some Web sites (particularly private sector-provided sites) mask advertising promotions and hyperlinks to their products and services in seemingly unbiased financial information and advice.

14. Including differing combinations of all delivery methods mentioned here.

15. In this category the OECD has included community/educational/debt advisory organisations.

16. In this category the OECD has included government-sponsored enterprises (GSEs) in the United States.

17. These include Austria's "Chambers of Labour" (Arbeiterkammern).

18. This group encompasses adolescents and students.

19. For more details related to this section, see Annex C.

20. Mallach summarises the Wilder Research Center's 1995 study findings on the Mortgage Foreclosure Prevention Program.

References

Bailey *et al.* (2002), "The Educational Desires of Financially Distressed Credit Counseling Clients", *Proceedings of the Association for Financial Counseling and Planning Education*, 2002, *www.ethomasgarman.net/research/feni/EducDesiresBailey.doc#*, accessed February 2005.

Boorstin, D., "Credit History: The Evolution of Consumer Credit in America", *The Ledger*, Federal Reserve Bank of Boston's Economic Education Newsletter, Spring/Summer 2004, *www.bos.frb.org/education/ledger/ledger04/sprsum/ sprsum04.pdf*, accessed February 2005.

Braunstein, S. and C. Welch (2002), "Financial Literacy: An Overview of Practice, Research and Policy", *Federal Reserve Bulletin*, Washington D.C., *www.federalreserve.gov/pubs/ bulletin/2002/1102lead.pdf#*, accessed 22 August 2003.

Citizens' Advice Bureau (CAB) (2001), *Summing Up: Bridging the Financial Literacy Divide*, *www.citizensadvice.org.uk/financialdivide.pdf*, accessed December 2004.

Debelle, G. (2004), "Macroeconomic implications of rising household debt", *Working Paper*, No. 153, Bank for International Settlements (BIS), Basel, Switzerland, *www.oenb.at/isaweb/report.do?&lang=EN&report=8.3.2*, accessed February 2005.

Durkin, T.A. (2000), "Credit Cards: Use and Consumer Attitudes, 1970-2000", *Federal Reserve Bulletin*, September 2000, Board of Governors of the Federal Reserve System, Washington D.C., *www.federalreserve.gov/pubs/bulletin/2000/0900lead.pdf*, accessed Febuary 2005.

Elliehausen, G.E., C. Lundquist and M.E. Staten (2002), "The Impact of Credit Counseling on Subsequent Borrower Credit Usage and Payment Behavior", Credit Research Center, *Monograph #36*, Georgetown University, *http://inchargefoundation.com/_assets/research_reports_and_publications/42.pdf*, accessed 27 June 2003.

Greenspan, A. (2003), "Financial Education", Speech given at the 33rd Annual Legislative Conference of the Congressional Black Caucus, Washington D.C., 26 September, *www.federalreserve.gov/boarddocs/speeches/2003/20030926/default.htm*, accessed February 2005.

Hamilton, R. (2003), "Trends in Households' Aggregate Secured Debt", *Quarterly Bulletin*, Autumn 2003, Bank of England, Bank of England Publications, London, United Kingdom, *www.bankofengland.co.uk/publications/quarterlybulletin/qb030301.pdf*, accessed February 2005.

Hirad, A. and P.M. Zorn (2001), "A Little Knowledge is a Good Thing: Empirical Evidence of the Effectiveness of Pre-Purchase Homeownership Counselling", paper presented at the conference on Sustainable Community Development; What Works, What Doesn't and Why, sponsored by the Federal Reserve System, Washington D.C., 27-28 March 2003, *www.chicagofed.org/cedric/files/2003_conf_paper_session1_zorn.pdf*, accessed February 2005.

Hopley, V. (2003), "Financial Education: What is it and What Makes it So Important?", *Community Reinvestment Report*, series, No. 1, Federal Reserve Bank of Cleveland, *www.clevelandfed.org/CommAffairs/CR_Reports/CRreport.pdf*, accessed 30 July 2003.

Jentzsch, N. (2003), "The Implications of the New Consumer Credit Directive for EU Credit Market Integration", *Position Paper*, Freie Universität Berlin, Berlin, *www.europarl.eu.int/hearings/20030429/juri/jentzsch1_en.pdf*, accessed February 2005.

Mallach, A. (no date), "Homeownership Education and Counseling: Issues in Research and Definition", *Community Affairs*, Federal Reserve Bank of Philadelphia, *www.phil.frb.org/cca/capubs/homeowner.pdf*, accessed February 2005.

Marcuss, M., (2004), "A Look at Household Bankruptcies", *Communities and Banking*, Spring 2004 issue, Federal Reserve Bank of Boston, *www.bos.frb.org/commdev/c&b/2004/Spring/Bankruptcies.pdf*, accessed March 2005.

Mavrinac, S. and C.W. Ping (2004), "Financial Education for Women in Asia Pacific", paper presented at the CITIGROUP/INSEAD Women's Financial Education Summit, 2 November 2004, Hong Kong, China, *www.insead.edu/discover_INSEAD/documents/WFEWorkingPaper.pdf*, accessed March 2005.

Murphy, R.G. (1999), "Household Debt and Aggregate Consumption Expenditures", *Boston College Working Papers in Economics*, No. 386, Boston College Department of Economics, *http://fmwww.bc.edu/EC-P/WP386.pdf*, accessed February 2005.

OECD (2000), *OECD Economic Outlook*, No. 68, December, OECD, Paris.

OECD (2004a), *Economic Survey of Korea*, Vol. 2004/10, OECD, Paris.

OECD (2004b), *OECD Economic Outlook*, No. 76, December, Annex Table 58, OECD, Paris.

Ogawa, K. and J. Wan (2004), "How Does Household Debt Affect Consumption? Evidence from MicroData", paper presented at the Micro Statistical Data Research Committee, 26 November 2004.

O'Neill, B. (2000), *How Clients Handle Money: Research Results and Implications*, Rutgers Cooperative Extension, State University of New Jersey at Rutgers, *www.rce.rutgers.edu/money/pdfs/handlemoney.pdf*, accessed 28 June 2004.

O'Neill, B. *et al.* (2000), "Money 2000: Feedback From and Impact on Participants", *Journal of Extension*, Vol. 38, No. 6, *www.joe.org/joe/2000december/rb3.html*, accessed 28 June 2004.

UK Department of Trade and Industry (UKDTI) and Department for Work and Pensions (UKDWP) (2004), *Tackling Over-Indebtedness Action Plan 2004*, United Kingdom, *www.dti.gov.uk/ccp/topics1/pdf1/overdebt0704.pdf*, accessed February 2005.

US Department of the Treasury, Office of Financial Education (2002), *Integrating Financial Education into School Curricula*, October 2002, *www.jumpstartcoalition.com/upload/treasurywhitepaper.pdf#*, accessed 25 June 2003.

ISBN 92-64-01256-7
Improving Financial Literacy
Analysis of Issues and Policies
© OECD 2005

Chapter 6

The Unbanked and Financial Education

In recent years, there has been growing concern in some OECD countries about financial exclusion and financial illiteracy, issues increasingly discussed in the context of wider debates about social inclusion and the profitability (and social responsibility) of financial institutions (Kempson et al., 2004; BBA, 2000; Connolly and Hajaj, 2001). Financial illiteracy can have a major impact on individuals' or households' daily money management, at the very least undermining their capacity to invest in key long-term goals (such as higher education, mortgages, retirement), at worst exposing them to severe financial crises. Focusing on four countries – Australia, Canada, United Kingdom and United States – this chapter begins by defining the unbanked and the types of consumers affected by financial exclusion, then discusses recent trends heightening the importance of the issue, the main causes and implications of the problem, and the growing importance of financial education initiatives in contributing to a solution.[1] Finally it gives an overview of existing financial education initiatives and the main policy implications for programme design. Despite the focus on the above four countries, it should be noted that the issues and programmes discussed in the chapter could apply to the least educated, disadvantaged and low-income populations in all OECD member and non-member countries.[2]

Background[3]

Consumers affected by financial exclusion and marginalisation are often called "unbanked" (without a bank account at a deposit institution) or "underserved" (rarely using their account, or not knowing how to use it). Although no precise figures or characteristics were found for underserved consumers (also referred to in the literature as "financially marginalised", "disadvantaged" or "vulnerable" consumers) they generally tend to have similar socio-economic and demographic profiles as the unbanked population. In all four countries, the unbanked and underserved populations are composed of heterogeneous and diverse consumer groups – such as, for example, low-income consumers, racial and ethnic minorities, immigrants, refugees and indigenous consumers – who tend to reside in either inner-city and deprived areas, or remote and isolated rural regions.

Demographic and market trends have contributed to greater financial exclusion. Higher birth rates among certain population groups (United States)[4] and greater immigration (United Kingdom) over past decades mean that more households of foreign origin now face language, educational, and cultural barriers to establishing a banking relationship, acquiring financial services and understanding economic complexities than before (Braunstein and Welch, 2002; NSUK, 2005).[5] Meanwhile, in the financial services sector, greater competition coupled with the demands of the majority are making the economics of cost-effective product and services provision to a minority more difficult as such provision is essentially less profitable (BBA, 2000). Thus, retail banks are increasingly focusing on their more profitable products and services, which typically results in the unbanked and underserved being left further behind (BBA, 2000). In some OECD countries, lack of access to financial services has been aggravated in recent years by a reduction in the number of banks (Stegman, 2003). One manifestation of this trend is the "reduced over-the-counter access" resulting from the closure of banks and post offices in Canada, the United Kingdom and Australia (Peachey and Roe, 2004; Connolly and Hajaj, 2001; Kempson et al., 2004). Simultaneously with these developments in the mainstream financial sector there has been a proliferation of nonbank or alternative financial service (AFS) providers such as check cashers and sub-prime and predatory lenders[6] who often target the unbanked.[7] In the United States, for example, the number of check-cashing centres has doubled over the past five years.[8] Australia, meanwhile, has seen damage done by sub-prime lending, particularly in its indigenous communities[9] (ECI, 2004).

These findings notwithstanding, research shows that while the unbanked populations are sometimes excluded by financial institutions, behavioural or psychological factors are often the major barriers to opening accounts (Kempson et al., 2004). These include seeing no need for or benefit of an account, lack of awareness about how to use or manage accounts, ignorance of the high wcosts incurred by not having a mainstream bank account, fear of or unfamiliarity with new electronic banking technologies – such as automated teller machines (ATMs), and misguided beliefs that traditional banks (and products) do not offer the specific services needed or set service charges too high. Such psychological and behavioural factors appear to be exacerbated by a lack of basic financial literacy skills (including poor basic numeracy and literacy skills), a lack of confidence in dealing with financial matters, a lack of familiarity with new electronic technologies, and/or past problems related to credit,[10] all combined with a fear, suspicion, and/or mistrust of banks and of the financial system in general. Other factors (most common among immigrants or indigenous peoples) include administrative complications – namely misunderstanding (or lack of) the types of necessary identity papers required; lack of physical access to bank branches or ATMs in remote areas; and specific religious beliefs or engrained cultural values that affect attitudes to mainstream borrowing or individual wealth accumulation.[11]

Finally, administrative changes at government level brought about by advanced technology, such as the move in the late 1990s in the United Kingdom and the United States to have all government payments made electronically, as well as the increasing requirement for individuals to be responsible for their own financial well-being that has accompanied welfare reforms, have contributed to heightening the importance of financial exclusion as a policy concern (Cruickshank, 2000; FRB, 2001; Kempson *et al.*, 2004; Reynolds, 2003; Stegman, 1998). Electronic government payments have made having a bank account essential in order to be able to receive state pay and benefits. In the light of these developments, it has become all the more important for unbanked consumers to access information about basic bank accounts, checking and savings accounts and other financial services, and to understand the fundamentals of account management. Financial education programmes are now required to enable unbanked and underserved citizens to access this information, and help them feel confident of their own economic capabilities and of their potential for financial self-sufficiency.

Benefits of financial education for the unbanked[12]

The OECD's research suggests that bringing more unbanked customers into the financial mainstream would lead to:

- Higher household savings levels, which in turn should have two advantages: a rise in savings levels in the economy and a fostering of home-buying and asset-building in communities. With no established banking relationship, the unbanked are forced to turn to relatively more expensive alternative financial services to transfer money and carry out other transactions. If more of these consumers were to reduce the high annual transaction costs associated with the use of AFS, there would be several beneficial ripple effects in the economy: consumers would ultimately possess more money for investments and savings and have a greater incentive to save simply because they have a bank account, leading to a rise in savings levels[13] (Stegman, 2003). Improved savings and higher levels of assets can be highly beneficial for low-income consumers both in the short term and the long term: in the short term they can act as a cushion against temporary crises, such as injury or job loss, and in the long term, they can result in increased savings for retirement and home-ownership. Moreover, on a wider scale, increased savings and asset-building have the potential to revitalise disadvantaged and impoverished communities (Barr, 2004).

- A greater number of consumers both covered by consumer protection laws and safeguarded against unfair, discriminatory practices (such as predatory lending).

- Cost savings for the Treasury and banks – through the reduced costs of electronic funds transfers, the resulting improved efficiency of payments delivery, and a reduced likelihood of fraud.[14]

- Enhanced business for financial institutions who would potentially gain millions of new customers.[15]

Research also highlights some examples of the benefits of financial education and literacy programmes for achieving these goals:

- Programmes can offer a better understanding of mainstream financial services and encourage the unbanked to avoid non-standard services. The result could be greater participation in the banking system among excluded consumers and an increased likelihood that, once in the system, they will more successfully manage the mainstream products (including basic checking, credit and savings accounts/instruments) they acquire (Braunstein and Welch, 2002). Financial education is, then, a potential solution to the problem of lack of access to financial services in unbanked and underserved communities.

- Second, initiatives informing unbanked and underserved consumers about the disadvantages of alternative financial services and the hazards of taking out high-risk loans can help them understand product risks and benefits, and help them see the advantages of holding mainstream checking and savings accounts. This would enable these consumers to make better decisions about their financial future and thus ultimately contribute to long-term reduction of harmful lending and improvement of asset-building in financially marginalised communities (Malkin, 2003).

- Finally, financial education programmes can lower the costs to unbanked and underserved consumers of becoming better informed about basic financial issues and of acquiring financial skills by providing more information on financial topics relevant to the un/underbanked as well as financial literacy instruction (helping them process this information and then enabling them to use it to make better informed decisions). With many of this group already on low incomes, reducing the costs of becoming better informed and acquiring skills is particularly important.

Description of current programmes on the unbanked[16]

Financial education programmes can be catalogued by target population (generic unbanked, underserved and low-income, immigrants and indigenous). In the four selected countries, the OECD identified some 109 financial education programmes suitable for the unbanked and underserved population.[17] They vary, broadly speaking, in target population, provider, delivery channel, content and aims.[18] The extent of the development of these programmes also varies across countries, with a considerable number of initiatives in the United Kingdom and the United States, and some in Canada established over the past decade, and a lesser number initiated more recently in Australia.

It is often difficult to obtain a clear-cut picture of the socio-economic/ demographic groups making up the primary target audience of programmes.

Most of the initiatives reviewed are intended for a heterogeneous audience likely to be composed of two or more groups. Some programmes are intended for basic bank account applicants or consumers with low educational levels. Several target low- and moderate-income consumer audiences, who might be one or a combination of the following: immigrants, ethnic minorities, refugees, low-income earners, inner-city dwellers, welfare recipients, indigenous, elderly and low-income first-time homebuyers. Increasingly it is being recognised that a one-size-fits-all approach cannot meet the specific needs of each unbanked and underserved population. Thus a growing number of programmes are being designed specifically for particular groups, such as minorities/immigrants or indigenous/rural communities. Finally a considerable number target the financial education trainers of the unbanked and underserved population (train-the-trainer programmes).

Many educational programmes are integrated into the provision of specific financial services, such as first or basic bank accounts, checking and savings accounts and matched-savings plans, while others adopt a broad stand-alone approach, teaching budgeting, savings and credit management, etc., with no connection to any product or service. Aims tend to vary according to the majority target population. For the generic unbanked, aims are to explain the benefits and use of bank account ownership and services or to build up fundamental financial literacy skills. For low/moderate-income underserved consumers, most programmes offer advice on general money and credit management; whereas others have a specific end goal or are embedded in schemes to encourage savings (such as IDAs),[19] asset-building and homeownership. These initiatives aim to build economic empowerment and increase long-term self-sufficiency in order to revitalise and stabilise disadvantaged neighbourhoods. A few have specific aims such as providing information to the working poor about tax credits, and enhancing access to banking services for the homeless or the elderly, for example. Programmes for minorities and immigrants are often embedded in other types of schemes, and have differing aims such as promotion of trust in the native banking system, integration into the adopted country, tackling lack of credit history or aiming to overcome religious-related barriers.[20] For indigenous or rural community programmes, goals include encouraging the use of electronic banking and fostering better management of income and credit.

Most of those programmes for which the OECD has been able to identify start dates were initiated in the late 1990s and the early 2000s. The United States accounts for the majority of the programmes identified, with most implemented at community or national level, and the remainder at municipal or state level. The United Kingdom accounts for the next highest number of programmes, the majority of which have national scope. Australia is responsible for approximately one-eighth of the programmes identified, with the majority at national level and the remainder at community or state level. Finally, Canada also offers a few programmes which are documented in part II.

The delivery channels for the programmes described above are (in order of frequency of use): training courses; followed by two or more delivery channels,[21] printed or online publications; advisory services (including telephone helplines and 1-to-1 counselling); Internet Web sites/online services,[22] public awareness-raising campaigns[23] and events (including lectures, national workshop/forum, symposia, presentations); and other methods (including resource packs, videos, computer programmes). It should be noted that some training courses contain a portion of one-on-one instruction and/or counselling, often parallel to workshops. Moreover, the courses tended to be provided in a traditional classroom setting, often using set, pre-designed curricula adapted to the majority demographic profile of their audience. Community outreach meetings and presentations are also occasional elements of the courses. Finally the majority of all the programmes targeted to minorities, immigrants, or refugees are offered both in English and in the population's native language, either through bilingual instructors or the availability of interpreters or translated written materials, and most programmes for indigenous adopt a delivery style sensitive to indigenous perceptions of wealth.

Providers vary greatly across the private and public sectors and tend to be (in order of frequency of use): non-profit/community/educational organisations; partnerships between two or more provider types (often consumer/community organisations and financial institutions); national government agencies/ departments or government-sponsored enterprises (GSEs); credit unions or credit union associations; financial regulatory and supervisory authorities; banks or financial institutions; and private sector companies.

Programmes for the unbanked and underserved have fairly complex funding arrangements, tending to pool together resources from across the public and private sectors.[24] Details of funding are available for 57 programmes. The majority of programmes have two or more funders for each initiative. A few initiatives use participant fees and programme revenues along with other sources of funding. Finally a small number of programmes also use volunteers to cut costs, but find it a challenge to obtain and retain enough interested volunteers.

Summary of evaluations of programmes on the unbanked[25]

The OECD was able to identify only three evaluation programmes: two in the United States and one in the United Kingdom, and all evaluating training courses. The evaluations offer some indications for the best and most cost-effective providers, planning, content and delivery methods for financial education to the un/underbanked. The main findings of these evaluations and the policy implications to be drawn from them can be summarised as follows:

With respect to providers, the United Kingdom-based evaluation endorses local provision to address financial literacy needs among the unbanked and underserved (Dartnall et al., 2002). According to the study, those best placed to reach the "hard-to-reach" are local community organisations who have already had wide-ranging experience in dealing with socially and financially excluded individuals, and in working with their own clients in local areas. Most significantly, they benefit from the trust, respect and confidence of the local community and can consolidate on these. In light of this, nonprofits – which are the majority provider across the 109 programmes identified by the OECD – would seem a suitable supplier of financial education programmes to the unbanked and underserved.

Where programme planning is concerned, with providers and instructors often coming from different organisations, problems are found to arise when the roles of these providers and instructors or aims of the programmes are uncertain (Dartnall et al., 2002). Thus there needs to be "clarity with regard to the aims" of any programme for the unbanked and underserved (Dartnall et al., 2002). There also must be consideration of the target population for programmes and of their particular concerns and needs. Where organisations are required to work in co-operation, whether at national or local level, those managing the programmes need to provide clear guidance , with the roles of each partner and lines of communication clarified.

With respect to the topics to be covered in programmes, some unbanked and underserved are overwhelmed with any provision of information about money management and financial literacy tools as they lack even basic literacy and numeracy skills. Others might have a minimum of basic skills but are financially illiterate. For a practical approach to this issue, the British-based evaluation suggests that courses be devised using a modular structure with two parts: a first module focusing on basic skills (through using finance-based examples, problems and issues) and a second module focusing more specifically on financial literacy and money management (Dartnall et al., 2002). This would mean that learners could attend either or both modules as appropriate.

Finally, both American and British evaluations discuss the best delivery methods for programmes and best choice of materials, venues and instructors. The British evaluation finds that training courses are important for effective learning, and it would seem significant that this is the most popular delivery channel of all 109 programmes identified by the OECD (Dartnall et al., 2002). Courses should use resources appropriate to adult learners, and be informally delivered in appropriate environments, with local trainers and incentives set (Dartnall et al., 2002). Where resources are concerned, uniquely paper-based materials are not found to be the most effective resource: it is recommended that materials be varied and, where possible, entertaining (videos, games, interactive exercises, handouts, etc.) (Dartnall *et al.*, 2002). With respect to environment or venue, evaluations find that courses and seminars work well in a classroom environment, preferably in a community or small group setting with a trusted community leader as instructor. It is essential that participants feel comfortable in the environment chosen for the course and that they learn better from a trainer with whom they are familiar or can trust (Anderson *et al.*, 2002). Small group settings also allow clients to work on individual learning plans and to develop their social skills as well as their financial literacy skills. Finally, the evaluations recommend that fixed incentives be set encouraging programme participants to learn and become more interested in financial matters. Other incentives could include certificates of completion and graduation ceremonies for concluding sessions (Anderson *et al.*, 2002).

Summary of policy implications for programmes on the unbanked

The literature and evaluations reviewed in this chapter offer some indications for effective provision of financial education to the unbanked and underserved population. Financial education programmes for these consumers should convince them about the benefits of being banked, and supply information about available banking services and appropriate training to assist them in opening their first bank accounts. Once they have opened these accounts, programmes should then provide ongoing financial and budget management training as an essential component to help the underserved make wiser financial choices. They should do this through the provision of instruction, information and objective advice to build the money management tools necessary for un/underbanked to effectively manage their accounts, and the financial understanding necessary to continue operating as successful accountholders, so rendering them more self-sufficient for the future. Financial education initiatives for un- and underbanked should thus have a preventive role, helping this population acquire the financial skills essential for independent participation in today's economy and thus enabling them to avoid, for example, the continued use of costly paper-based methods and alternative financial services, or having to resort to state assistance.

Financial education programmes clearly have the potential to help policymakers resolve the complexities of financial exclusion and marginalisation. This is particularly true when the lack of understanding about finance among this population is taken into account, both as a symptom and an underlying cause of many of the problems outlined thus far, and leading to the financial exclusion that these problems perpetuate. The provision of programmes for the un/underbanked group can thus play three important roles: firstly they can encourage un/underbanked consumers to enter into or make better use of the financial mainstream, secondly they can help to retain them as successful accountholders in the short-term, and thirdly they can contribute to keeping them there as savers for the long term. Thus these programmes can encourage the un- and under-banked to overcome the barriers deterring them from using mainstream financial systems, and can build sustainable solutions to counteract the negative consequences of not having a bank account.

More detailed information on The Unbanked and Financial Education can be found in Annex D.

Notes

1. These four countries were chosen because they either provided information about programmes for the unbanked in response to the OECD's questionnaires on financial education or have an extensive literature documenting financial education initiatives for the unbanked.

2. The OECD also found limited information on financial exclusion in Belgium, France, Germany and Ireland. (Peachey and Roe, 2004; Kempson et al., 2004). One of the factors influencing financial exclusion is access to banks or similar financial institutions. It can be noted in this respect that in a bank-based financial system, as is the case in most continental European countries, there is likely to be a widespread network of banks.

3. For more details related to this section, see Annex D.

4. www.ncpa.org/pd/social/sociala.html.

5. Non-native groups tend to lack access to mainstream financial systems, may be unfamiliar with native financial practices and/or may not speak the native language.

6. Subprime lenders are lenders that accept low client credit scores, i.e. high-risk borrowers; predatory lenders are illegal lenders practising a type of loan fraud. (For more information, see Chapter 5 and Annex C.)

7. AFS providers charge unbanked clients higher fees for completing transactions than mainstream banks would charge their account-holders for equivalent transactions, and AFS annual fees far exceed the cost of maintaining mainstream checking/savings accounts (Caskey, 2002).

8. www.fisca.org.

9. Also www.asic.gov.au.

10. Past problems related to credit invariably require customers to close their accounts. Research in the United Kingdom, for example, shows that approximately one in six unbanked individuals who had a bank account in the past were forced to stop using it after finding themselves in financial difficulties (BBA, 2000).

11. The native American and Australian indigenous communities, for example, prefer to focus on increasing the assets of their community rather than individual asset-building (Malkin, 2003).

12. For more details related to this section, see Annex D.

13. Research finds a high correlation between bank account ownership and saving (Vermilyea and Wilcox, 2002 cited Barr and Sherraden, 2004).

14. In the United Kingdom, for example, Automated Credit Transfer (ACT) implemented in 1999 was estimated to be likely to save the government and British taxpayers approximately GBP 500 million annually through reduced administrative costs and GBP 100 million annually in reduced fraud (UKDSS, 2001).

15. With the numbers of unbanked totalling around 14.5 to 15.5 million individuals in the United States and the United Kingdom alone, financial institutions and markets have the potential to gain millions of new customers. (Here the combined sum of the figures for unbanked individuals previously cited in this chapter – 12 million in the United States, 2.5 to 3.5 million in the United Kingdom – has been calculated.)

16. For more details related to this section, see Annex D.

17. But this number is by no means exhaustive.

18. Unless otherwise indicated, information on financial education programmes on the unbanked comes from responses of the CMF delegates to the OECD's questionnaire on financial education.

19. Individual Development Account programmes: these aim to encourage low-income consumers to save by helping them establish saving accounts and by matching their deposits (http://gwbweb.wustl.edu/csd/asset/idas.htm). The IDAs have a financial literacy component that has contributed significantly to their success. Welfare assistance programmes might also benefit from similar, appropriately targeted, financial literacy components.

20. For example, the Web site of the Islamic Mortgage Initiative provided by government housing agency, Freddie Mac offers information on the functioning of this particular product meeting the home financing needs of a religious minority and aiming to improve Muslim access to mainstream financial services (www.freddiemac.com/homeownership/features/muslim_1106.htm).

21. Including differing combinations of all delivery methods mentioned here.

22. Care was taken to select only those Web sites/online services offering objective and unbiased information and advice. The OECD found during its research, that although not always obvious, some Web sites (particularly private sector-provided sites) mask adverts, promotions and hyperlinks to their products and services in seemingly unbiased financial information and advice.

23. Mainly delivered through lobbying, publicity, posters, publications, and media channels.

24. Government agencies or GSEs, non-profits, credit counselling agencies, Community Extension Service, financial institutions and banks, companies, private sector foundations.

25. For more details related to this section, see Annex D.

References

Anderson, S.G., J. Scott and M. Zhan (2002), Executive Summary of Financial Links for Low-Income People, (FLLIP): Evaluation of Implementation and Initial Training Activity, School of Social Work, University of Illinois at Urbana-Champaign, *www.povertylaw.org/advocacy/community_investment/executive_summary.doc*, accessed December 2004.

Barr, M.S. (2004), "Banking the Poor", *Yale Journal on Regulation*, Vol. 21, pp. 121-237, Winter 2004.

Barr, M.S. and M. Sherraden (2004), "Institutions and Inclusion in Saving Policy", paper presented at Building Assets, Building Credit: A Symposium on Improving Financial Services in Low-Income Communities, Harvard University, 18-19 November 2003, *www.jchs.harvard.edu/publications/finance/babc/babc_04-15.pdf*, accessed January 2005.

Braunstein, S. and C. Welch (2002), "Financial Literacy: An Overview of Practice, Research and Policy", Federal Reserve Bulletin, Washington D.C., *www.federalreserve.gov/pubs/bulletin/2002/1102lead.pdf#*, accessed 22 August 2003.

British Bankers' Association (BBA) (2000), Promoting Financial Inclusion – The Work of the Banking Industry, *www.bba.org.uk/content/1/c4/18/43/promoting2000.pdf*, accessed November 2004.

Caskey, J.P. (2002), "Bringing Unbanked Households into the Banking System", Capital Xchange, January 2002, *www.brook.edu/es/urban/capitalxchange/article10.htm*, accessed December 2004.

Connolly, C. and K. Hajaj (2001), Financial Services and Social Exclusion, Financial Services Consumer Policy Centre, University Of New South Wales, Chifley Research Centre, *www.chifley.org.au/publications/banking_and_social_exclusion_final_report.pdf*, accessed December 2004.

Cruickshank, D. (2000), Competition in UK Banking, Her Majesty's Stationery Office, London, UK *www.hm-treasury.gov.uk/documents/financial_services/banking/bankreview/fin_bank_reviewfinal.cfm*, accessed December 2004.

Dartnall, L. *et al.* (2002), Evaluation of the Community Development Programme in Financial Literacy and Basic Skills, National Foundation for Educational Research (NFER), *www.basic-skills.co.uk#*, accessed 16 July 2003.

ECI Africa Consulting (ECI) (2004), FinMark Trust: Financial Literacy Scoping Study and Strategy Report, *www.finmarktrust.org.za/documents/2004/AUGUST/FinLit_Report.pdf*, accessed December 2004.

Federal Reserve Board (FRB) (2001), "The Unbanked – Who Are They?", Capital Connections newsletter, Vol. 3, No. 2, *www.federalreserve.gov/dcca/newsletter/2001/spring01/unbank.htm* accessed December 2004.

Kempson, E., A. Atkinson and O. Pilley (2004), Policy Level Response To Financial Exclusion In Developed Economies: Lessons For Developing Countries, Personal Finance Research Centre, University of Bristol, Bristol, commissioned by Financial Sector Team, Policy Division, Department for International Development, UK, *www.microfinancegateway.org/files/21955_dfid_report.pdf* , accessed October 2004.

Malkin, J. (2003), "Financial Education in Native Communities: A Briefing Paper", paper presented at the Native American Financial Literacy Coalition's Financial Education in Native Communities national policy development forum, 28-29 May 2003, Denver, Colorado, *www.cfed.org/publications/Financial%20Education%20in%20Native%20Communities.pdf*, accessed 26 August 2003.

National Statistics United Kingdom (NSUK) (2005), "UK population grows to 59.6 million", 28 January, *www.statistics.gov.uk/cci/nugget.asp?id=760*, accessed March 2005.

Peachey, S. and A. Roe (2004), "Access To Finance: A Study For The World Savings Banks Institute", paper presented at the World Savings Banks Institute (WSBI) and World Bank International Access to Finance Conference, 28-29 October 2004, Brussels.*www.savings-banks-events.org/atf/programme.htm*,

Reynolds, F. (2003), "Promoting financial inclusion", Poverty 114, Journal of the Child Poverty Action Group, London, UK, *www.cpag.org.uk/info/Povertyarticles/Poverty114/financial.htm*, accessed December 2004.

Stegman, M.A. (1998), "Electronic Benefit's Potential to Help the Poor", Policy Brief, No. 32, The Brookings Institution, Washington D.C., *www.brookings.org/printme.wbs?page=/comm/policybriefs/pb32.htm*, accessed December 2004.

Stegman, M.A. (2003), "Banking the Unbanked: Connecting Residents of Social Housing to the Financial Mainstream", in R. Forrest and J. Lee (eds.), Housing and Social Change: East-West Perspectives, Routledge, London, *www.kenan-flagler.unc.edu/assets/documents/CC_Routledge-2003%20BankingUnbanked.pdf*, accessed December 2004.

UK Department of Social Security (UKDSS) [now known as the Department for Work and Pensions] (2001), Memorandum (PAC 00-01/70) concerning the Comptroller and Auditor General's Report of 18 August 2000, submitted by the Department Of Social Security to the Committee of Public Accounts, UK Parliament, 10 January, *www.publications.parliament.uk/pa/cm200001/cmselect/cmpubacc/282/1022602.htm*, accessed December 2004.

Internet References

Australian Securities and Investment Commission: [*www.asic.gov.au*] (accessed December 2004).

Center for Social Development, George Warren Brown School of Social Work, Washington University: [*http://gwbweb.wustl.edu/csd/*] (accessed December 2004).

Financial Service Centers of America, Inc.: [*www.fisca.org*] (accessed February 2005).

Freddie Mac: [*www.freddiemac.com*] (accessed March 2005).

National Center for Policy Analysis: [*www.ncpa.org*] (accessed February 2005).

ISBN 92-64-01256-7
Improving Financial Literacy
Analysis of Issues and Policies
© OECD 2005

Chapter 7

Conclusions and Future Directions for Financial Education

Most OECD countries are offering a variety of financial education programmes on a wide range of issues. In fact, in some countries, there are so many financial education programmes that there is concern about information overload for consumers. A number of countries have undertaken financial literacy surveys. And some countries have given considerable thought to evaluating financial education programmes and to identifying the characteristics of effective financial education programmes. A few countries consider financial education so important that they are developing national strategies to coordinate and direct their financial education programmes. But in relatively few countries have actual evaluations of financial education programmes been conducted. And most of these evaluations have taken place in just one country.

One major finding is that countries provide financial education in a variety of forms, ranging from the distribution of brochures and pamphlets on selected financial issues to the offering of training courses or conducting media campaigns. The most frequently used way of providing financial education is through Web sites. Most OECD countries have internet Web sites offering financial education, whether provided by public or private agencies. The next most used method is through the provision of brochures and publications. Though less frequently used than the above mentioned channels, courses and seminars are also used to deliver financial education. In some cases, correspondence courses, designed for adults, are available and essay competitions for students are held to encourage young people to get interested in financial management. A few countries have undertaken median campaigns to promote financial education. Countries also provide financial education on a wide range of issues, including credit, insurance, investment and pensions. Much of this information is directed to the general public although some of it is targeted more specifically to investors, consumers burdened with debt, or those individuals outside of the financial system. However, it is not clear to what extent the financial information presented to consumers takes into account the variability across consumers in financial understanding.[1]

Another finding is that, despite the emphasis of policymakers on financial education programmes, few countries have undertaken financial literacy surveys to determine which financial issues are of most concern and need for consumers. Those surveys that have been undertaken indicate that many consumers do not

IMPROVING FINANCIAL LITERACY – ISBN 92-64-01256-7 – © OECD 2005

have an adequate financial background or understanding. Eleven OECD countries have conducted financial literacy surveys and three are planning to conduct such surveys. Despite the differences across these surveys in terms of target audience, approach to measuring financial literacy, and survey methodology, there are a number of similarities in the results. One result common to all the surveys is the low level of financial understanding among consumers. The surveys that ask questions about consumer demographics find that financial understanding is correlated with education and income levels, although highly educated consumers with high incomes can be just as ignorant about financial issues as less educated, lower income consumers. Another common result is that consumers often believe they know more about financial matters than is actually the case, beliefs that can lead to financial trouble. These surveys also indicate that consumers have difficulty in finding and understanding financial information.

A third finding is that there have been few evaluations of financial education programmes to determine what has worked well and what has not. This is in part due to the fact that programme evaluation is expensive and government budgets are limited. But equally important is the difficulty of coming up with feasible measures of the goals of the financial education programme: increasing consumer awareness and changing individual financial behaviour. Many of the evaluations that this report identified are found in employer-provided financial education programmes targeted at workers. Here measures of behaviour change are easier to identify. Employers collect data on participation in pension plans, contribution levels, and asset allocations. Consequently, the effectiveness of financial education programmes can be measured in terms of the extent to which workers have increased participation and contribution levels and changed asset allocations in the desired direction. However, when financial information is provided through Web sites or brochures distributed in public places, it is difficult to develop effective measures of behaviour change. For example, there is no way to know if those who accessed a Web site or picked up a brochure understood what they read and/or changed their behaviour as a result. In the case of financial education courses, participants can be evaluated both before and after the course to measure the increase in understanding of financial concepts as a result of the course. However, to truly measure the effectiveness of the course, measures of behaviour change would have to be devised.[2]

A related finding is that, where evaluated, financial education programmes have been found to be effective. Research in the United States shows that workers increase their participation in and contributions to 401(k) plans when employers offer financial education, whether in the form of brochures or seminars. Financial education in the form of mortgage counselling has been found to be effective in reducing the risks of mortgage delinquency. Consumers who attend one-on-one credit counselling sessions have lower debt and fewer delinquencies than consumers who do not. More subjective evaluations of financial education programmes for the unbanked have found that participants are satisfied with the training they received and are more confident about making financial decisions.

Finally, as important as it might potentially be to improving financial literacy of consumers, financial education might not always be the most effective approach to improving consumer well-being. Research in behavioural finance has identified a number of psychological traits that militate against the success of financial education. For example, according to surveys a significant proportion of consumers lack the discipline to set and adhere to savings goals. Others are overwhelmed by the large number of financial instruments available and therefore do not purchase any. In the area of pensions this has led many experts to argue for automatic enrolment for defined contribution plans along with default contribution rates and default asset allocations. Some research has shown that such approaches are more effective than financial education alone in raising retirement savings. However, most experts also acknowledge that financial education still has a role to play in providing advice and information to workers about their retirement plans.

What the report makes clear, however, is that there is much more to do and learn about financial education programmes and how to make them better. First, it is important to increase consumer awareness as to the necessity of financial education and how they can access it. Financial education is not just for investors. It is just as important, if not more so, for the average family trying to balance its budget and save for the children's education and the parent's retirement. More needs to be learned about the financial education needs of consumers at various stages in their lives and how financial education programmes can be designed and implemented to best address these needs. How can financial education programmes better reach those consumers that most need them? More needs to be learned about how consumers prefer to receive information on financial issues. How can financial education programmes be best delivered to consumers busy with jobs and families? Objective measures identifying programme success need to be developed and more evaluations of programmes need to be conducted. Ideally, more information needs to be gathered on individual programmes in order to more confidently produce a list of good practices. More research and more evaluation are necessary. Currently it is not possible to compare financial literacy across countries nor even to compare it over time within a country. In addition, data on savings rates, household debt, and changes in pension coverage are difficult to find in the detail necessary to allow a critical comparison across countries.

This book focuses on programmes that are offered outside of schools. Research for the current study indicates, however, that it is important to educate individuals as early as possible about financial issues. Consequently, a next stage of the project, which would be developed in cooperation with the Education Directorate, would describe and analyse financial education programmes available in schools and universities. This second stage of the project would result in a major report on financial literacy among young people and the state of financial education in schools.

The OECD will also develop further work on financial education and awareness with respect to insurance and pensions. The research in this book will be extended to examine in more detail the important role of financial education in increasing consumers' awareness and understanding of insurance issues, including the benefits of insurance coverage. Another extension of the research presented in this book will focus on the role of financial education in both defined benefit and defined contribution pension schemes and the development of appropriate guidelines on financial education for retirement savings.

Notes

1. While many countries offer financial education programmes, some countries have opted for a regulatory-based approach. These countries see the role of government as ensuring that financial advisors have a certain minimum level of competence and that consumers are provided with accurate and unbiased financial information. In this case the burden of protecting the consumer is placed on the providers of financial services. Although this approach is not developed further in the present report, this option needs to be kept in mind by policymakers, as it offers an alternative and a possible complement to financial education.

2. The measures of effectiveness used would depend upon the goals of the course, *e.g.* whether the point of the course was to provide basic information about setting up a bank account, to help people their level of debt, or to start saving for retirement. For example, if the course were on saving, questions could be asked about whether the attendees had opened up a savings account or increased contributions to an already existing account. Data would then have to be collected both before and at several points after the course in order to determine if behaviour had actually changed.

ISBN 92-64-01256-7
Improving Financial Literacy
Analysis of Issues and Policies
© OECD 2005

ANNEX A

Assessment of Financial Literacy of Consumers: Additional Information

Assessment of existing financial literacy surveys

Surveys using objective measures

The surveys in the United States and Korea are based on a questionnaire developed by the Jumpstart Coalition for Personal Literacy.[1] The survey has been conducted four times in the United States (1997, 2000, 2002 and 2004) and once in Korea (2000).[2] The target group in Korea is 10th and 11th graders; in the United States the target group is high school students in 12th grade. The survey consists of multiple choice questions and, in the case of the United States, is administered in English or history classes that do not focus on finance or economics, in order to ensure a representative group of students. The sample of students is selected so as to be representative of the population of 12th graders in public schools.[3]

The questionnaire was designed by a team of educators and consists of approximately 50 questions of which 20 ask for demographic information and 30 measure students' understanding of personal finance basics in four areas: income, money management, savings and investment, and spending and debt. With respect to income, the questions test students' ability to analyse the impact of personal choices, such as education, on future income, to identify sources of income, and to explain how disposable income is affected by personal taxes and transfer payments. With respect to financial management, the questions test students' ability to identify the opportunity costs of financial decisions, to establish and evaluate goals with respect to income and saving, to develop a budget, to explain relationships among taxes, income, spending and investing, and to develop a risk management plan the includes the appropriate types of insurance. With respect to savings and investments, the questions test students' ability to compare the advantages and disadvantages of saving early *versus* saving later, to explain the importance of short and long-term saving and investment strategies, to identify and evaluate the risk, return and liquidity of various financial instruments, and to explain how saving and investment decisions are affected by taxes, government policy, and inflation. With respect to expenditure and debt, the questions test students' ability to compare the advantages and disadvantages of spending now *versus* spending later, to evaluate the benefits and costs of using different means of payment such as cash, checks and credit cards, to explain how the risk level of the borrower affects the price of credit, to explain the relationship between payment performance and credit history, to explain the rights and responsibilities of buyers, sellers and creditors, to use cost benefit analysis to choose among spending alternatives, and to analyse the best ways to deal with financial difficulties (Mandell, 2001).

Surveys using subjective measures

The surveys conducted by Australia, Japan and the United Kingdom are essentially surveys of opinion and ask primarily about respondents' views with respect to ownership of financial products, about how they acquire information on financial products, about their views on the importance of financial education, and about their awareness of the financial environment.

Australia conducted a survey of adults in 2002-03 (ANZ Banking Group, 2003).[4] This is a two-part survey in which a national random sample of 3 548 adults was interviewed by phone and 202 adults in Sydney and Melbourne were interviewed in depth, in part to investigate issues raised in the telephone survey. Those telephoned were asked both finance questions and demographic questions. Out of a total of 145 finance questions and 25 demographic questions, all respondents were asked a number of core questions. Other questions were either asked only if relevant (*e.g.* if respondent owned a credit card) or were randomly allocated to a 50 per cent subsample of respondents, so as to minimise the number of questions asked. Individuals were questioned only on the issues relevant to their needs and circumstances and not on the entire array of financial products and services, some of which they might neither use nor need.

The Australian survey, like the Jumpstart survey, identifies a number of topics about which consumers should be knowledgeable. This survey attempts to measure the extent to which Australians have basic mathematical and reading and comprehension skills in addition to measuring financial understanding, financial competence, and financial responsibility. By financial understanding is meant that consumers understand what money is, how it is exchanged, and where it comes from and where it goes. Under financial competence, consumers need to understand the main features of basic financial services, to understand financial records and appreciate the importance of reading and retaining them, to be aware that some financial products have risk and to appreciate the relationship between risk and return. Financial responsibility includes the ability to make appropriate personal life choices about financial issues, the understanding of consumer rights and responsibilities, and the ability and confidence to access assistance when things go wrong. Because this survey asks questions that test respondents' financial knowledge as well as questions about their perceptions of financial issues, the results can be used to compare how consumers feel about financial issues with how knowledgeable they are about them.

The Central Council for Financial Services Information in Japan sponsors two consumer surveys dealing with financial issues, the Public Opinion Survey on Household Financial Assets and Liabilities and the Consumer Survey on Finance. The former has been conducted annually since 1953 (Central Council, 2002). The most recent results available in English are for the 2002 survey, which was conducted between June 21 and July 1 of that year. Six thousand households were included in the survey and 4 149 households responded, a response rate of 69.2%. These 6 000 households were selected based on a stratified two-stage random sampling method. Interviewers visited the selected households and left a questionnaire to be filled out. Several days later the interviewers returned and collected the completed questionnaires. This survey asks questions about the ownership of financial products, savings and risk, the deposit insurance system, incomes and expenditures, amount of outstanding debt, financial life planning, and life in old age. The second survey is the Consumer Survey on Finance.[5] This survey has to date been conducted twice, once in 2001 and again in 2003. The 2001 sample, for which results are available in English, included 4 000 men and women across the country who were 20 years or older. Of these 4 000, 2 638 responded for a response rate of 66 per cent. Respondents were asked about their knowledge of finance, financial products, and financial issues. They were also asked about financial information provided by various organisations and companies, about the kind of financial information and knowledge that is useful in their daily lives, about the type of financial information they want to have, about their main sources of financial information and knowledge and about how they think this information and knowledge should be provided.

In the United Kingdom, the Financial Services Authority sponsored a survey of adults that was conducted by BMRB International Limited between June 28 and July 18, 1999 (FSA, 2000). The target audience was adults and 1 081 individuals were interviewed in face-to-face interviews. A random location sampling design, a sophisticated form of quota sampling, was used to select the sample. The demographic profile in the sample matches that in the adult population. Prior to this survey, qualitative research was carried out to help design the questionnaire for the survey and to further investigate the financial information needs of certain subgroups of consumers. This qualitative research was conducted in May 1999. It involved 16 individual in-depth interviews, six mini-groups (with four to six respondents each) and eight focus groups with seven to nine respondents each. Interviewees were asked questions to identify their information needs with respect to financial products, how they got their information about these products, their willingness to use different sources of information and advice, their attitudes about financial matters, their confidence in dealing with financial matters, and their use of financial products.

Results

Although the surveys differed in target audience, approach to measuring financial literacy, and survey methodology, there are a number of similarities in the results.

- One result common to all the surveys is the low level of financial understanding among consumers.
- The surveys that ask about consumer demographics find that financial understanding is correlated with education and income levels.
- Another result common across surveys is that respondents often feel they know more about financial matters than is actually the case.
- Surveys also note that consumers feel financial information is difficult to find and understand.

All the surveys find low levels of financial literacy among consumers

The surveys in the United States and Korea that use objective tests to measure financial literacy find that students have only a limited grasp of financial basics. In the Korean survey, in no category do the students answer more than 50 per cent of the questions correctly. The scores for American students are not much better. On tests designed to measure students' ability to choose and manage a credit card, knowledge to save and invest for retirement, and awareness of risk and the importance of insuring against it – basic financial decisions – the students in these two countries have failing scores. This at a time when an increasing number of students use credit cards, the responsibility for saving for retirement is increasingly falling on the individual, and the financial costs of being uninsured are rising.

Table A.1 compares the scores of American and Korean students in four different categories of financial information as presented in the JumpStart surveys administered in the year 2003 in Korea and 2000 in the United States. Students in both countries score highest when asked about income issues, with the Korean students having an average score of 48.7 per cent (out of 100) and the American students having an average score of 57.6 per cent (out of 100). Neither

Table A.1. **Comparison of literacy scores: Korean and American students**

Category	Average score	
	Korea (2003)	United States (2000)
Income	48.7	57.6
Financial management	39.2	46.8
Savings and investment	46.6	45.3
Expenditure and debt	44.0	52.1

Source: Korea – Response to OECD questionnaire on financial education, July 2003. United States – L. Mandell (2001), *Improving Financial Literacy: What Schools and Parents Can and Cannot Do*, The Jumpstart Coalition for Personal Financial Literacy, Washington D.C.

of these scores is a passing grade on a scale in which 60 to 69 is a D, 70 to 79 a C, etc. The Korean students score lowest on financial management while the American students score lowest on savings and investment.

Low as these scores are, analysts point out that these results actually understate the lack of financial literacy. The sample in the United States excludes high school dropouts and includes less than two per cent who planned no additional education. Had these students been included, scores would have been even lower. In addition, a number of questions test knowledge of terminology rather than reasoning ability. Had more of the questions asked about reasoning ability, scores would have been lower (Mandell, 2001).

Surveys in both countries also ask questions to determine if experience or knowledge about money management has an effect on students' scores. The expectation is that students who discuss money matters with their parents, receive a regular allowance, or have bank accounts and/or stocks, will have a better understanding of financial issues. If this were the case, it would suggest that possible ways to increase the financial literacy of students would be to encourage them to talk to their parents about financial issues, get a particular type of bank account or purchase stock, etc. Unfortunately, discussions with one's parents about money, the receipt of a regular allowance, or the ownership of financial products do not necessarily translate into financial understanding.

In both countries students receive failing scores despite discussions about financial issues with their parents, receipt of a regular allowance, or ownership of financial products. However, in both countries, students who discuss financial matters with their parents have higher scores than students who do not, as shown in Table A.2. The receipt of an allowance on a regular basis, as opposed to periodically or when necessary, does not have a positive effect on literacy scores in the United States and only a small effect in Korea. Interestingly, the type of bank account is related to scores on the test and differs by country. American students with savings accounts score significantly higher than those with only checking accounts or no bank

Table A.2. **Results by money management experience and education**

	Korea (2003)		United States (2000)	
	% of students	Mean score	% of students	Mean score
A. Where students learned most about money management				
Family	50.2	46.4	57.4	51.8
School	5.0	37.2	12.8	51.3
Friends	8.3	41.7	2.1	35.6
Magazines, books, TV	13.6	47.6	3.4	53.7
Personal experience	22.0	44.2	23.0	53.5
B. Discuss money matters with parents				
Never	13.8	40.9	6.7	42.5
Rarely	33.3	45.5	18.2	52.4
Sometimes	41.4	46.6	39.1	52.6
Often	10.9	44.6	34.7	52.6
C. Allowance				
When necessary	47.6	45.8	52.5	51.9
Periodically	5.9	37.1	35.3	51.6
Regularly	35.8	47.4	10.5	48.9
Never	9.7	39.0	–	–
D. Bank account				
None/don't know	13.2	38.5	37.8	49.3
Savings only	8.4	40.6	41.0	53.8
Checking only	56.2	47.5	7.3	45.6
Savings and checking	21.1	45.3	18.2	54.9
E. Security ownership				
None	75.2	47.7	75.3	52.6
Stocks in own name	4.8	35.4	9.2	52.7
Mutual fund in own name	3.5	29.8	4.7	52.2

Source: Korea – Response to OECD questionnaire on financial education, July 2003. United States – L. Mandell (2001), Improving Financial Literacy: What Schools and Parents Can and Cannot Do, The Jumpstart Coalition for Personal Financial Literacy, Washington D.C.

account at all. One explanation is that those students with savings accounts are "more aware of the value of saving as part of an overall financial plan" (Mandell, 2001). In Korea, though, it is students with a checking account who score the highest. Security ownership has little effect on students' scores, whether in Korea or the United States. This result might be explained by the fact that so few students own either stocks or bonds. In addition, the American survey finds that students who play an interactive stock market game in class have an average score four percentage points higher than the scores of those students who do not. Thus, these findings suggest that some practical strategies for improving literacy may be effective, although not effective enough to ensure passing scores.

The results from these surveys do need to be viewed with some caution, however. For example, according to both the 2000 and the 2002 surveys in the United States, students who have an entire course in personal finance or in economics do slightly worse than average on the exam. However, in the 2004 survey students in schools where money management courses are required do slightly better than students in schools where such courses are either not required for all students or are elective. These differing results over time suggest that more research is needed in this area.

Finally, the US survey has recorded declining levels of financial literacy over time. The percentage of questions answered correctly is highest the first year the survey was conducted in 1997. The percentages have been lower in subsequent years, although the decline that began in 2000 appears to have been reversed in 2004.

Table A.3. **Literacy scores over time: United States**

% of questions answered correctly

2004	52.3
2002	50.2
2000	51.9
1997	57.3

Source: L. Mandell (2004), 2004 Personal Finance Survey of High School Seniors, executive summary, The Jumpstart Coalition for Personal Financial Literacy, Washington D.C.

The surveys using subjective measures of financial literacy also find that many consumers have a limited understanding of financial issues. For example, the two Japanese surveys find that significant proportions of respondents admit knowing little about such basic financial issues as risks related to investment, measures of consumer protection, or interest rates. For example, 76 per cent of the respondents to the Consumer Survey on Finance say that they have almost no knowledge about risks relating to investment, 71 per cent say they have almost no knowledge about investment in equities and bonds, 65 per cent say they have no knowledge about consumer protection such as the deposit insurance system, and 57 per cent say they have no knowledge of financial products in general. This survey also finds there is a high rate of ignorance for relatively common financial products. For example, 29 per cent say they have no knowledge about insurance, pensions, and tax and 23 per cent say they have no knowledge about savings and deposits.

> ### Box A.1. **Financial literacy in the United States: another survey**
>
> The low levels of financial literacy observed in the Jumpstart Survey are corroborated in a survey conducted in 1999 by Louis Harris and Associates for the National Council on Economic Education. This survey examines the familiarity of both students and adults with basic economic principles, knowledge of the US economy, and understanding of some key economic terms. Half of all adults and two-thirds of high school students fail the test on basic economics that is part of the survey. Almost 40 per cent of adults and students think the statement "Money holds its value well in times of inflation" is correct. More than a third of students admit they do not know what the effect of an increase in interest rates would be on savings. Many of the questions asked deal with recognition of terms or concepts rather than application of these concepts to particular situations. Thus, these scores might well be lower if respondents had been asked to apply what they know to specific situations (NCEE, 1999).

Seventy per cent of respondents to the Japanese Public Opinion Survey on Household Financial Assets and Liabilities do not know about investors' protection funds, which are designed to protect securities investors' assets held in custody by a securities company's custody up to 10 million yen per investor. Although 78 per cent know that the deposit insurance system protects bank deposits up to 10 million yen,[6] only 14 per cent know that Japanese branches of foreign banks not headquartered in Japan are not covered and only 21 per cent know that foreign currency deposits and investment trusts are not covered. This survey also finds little awareness of interest rates. This is in 2002, at a time when interest rates were very low in Japan and had been for some time. Up until early in 2001 the official interest rate was half a per cent. In 2001 it fell to almost zero. Yet, sixty-five per cent of respondents say they have taken no particular actions in response to current interest rate conditions, while 12 per cent say they switched to financial products expected to yield higher interest or return and 19 per cent say they decided to hold cash temporarily or to spend their savings on consumption goods.

The Australian survey notes that consumers in that country have a limited grasp of certain financial fundamentals.[7] Of those who receive and read their superannuation statement, 21 per cent report that they do not understand it. When respondents are asked to answer four questions about a sample statement, only 49 per cent answer all four questions correctly. In fact, 29 per cent of respondents cannot identify asset allocation from a superannuation statement and 38 per cent cannot identify the five-year investment performance from the same statement. Only 37 per cent of Australian respondents have determined how much they will actually need to save for retirement. Only 19 per cent have used an Internet calculator to compare the effects of interest rates and fees on investments. Finally, 32 per cent of respondents think that saving money in a bank account is an appropriate retirement investment vehicle.

The surveys find that financial understanding is correlated with education and income levels

All the surveys ask demographic questions, that is, questions about the respondent's gender, age, income level, education, etc. Given this information it is possible to determine how financial literacy varies with demographic characteristics.

The surveys find that there is a strong correlation between financial literacy and socio-economic status. In Australia, for example, the lowest levels of financial literacy are associated with low levels of education (year 10 or less), unemployment or low skilled work, low incomes (household income under $20 000), low levels of savings (under $5 000), being single, and being at either end of the age profile (18-24 year olds and those aged 70 years or older). More detail is shown in Table A.4.

In the United Kingdom, individuals in the lower social grades and the lowest income band, as well as young people aged 18 to 24, are found to be the least receptive consumers – uninterested, unconfident, and least active. In contrast, the higher social grades, those with higher income, young couples and older respondents with no family are sophisticated financial consumers and understand how to get the information they need and understand the advice they receive.

In the Korean and American surveys, scores broken down by demographic characteristics indicate that students from families with less educated parents and low income and professional expectations score the lowest. However, there are some differences between Korea and the United States with respect to the impact of these demographic characteristics. In Korea, family monthly income does not seem to have an effect unless it is very low. In the United States, family income does have a significant effect on students' scores. The effect of parents' education is also more noticeable in the United States than in Korea. Higher levels of expected salary coincide with higher scores in the United States but not in Korea. Students who plan to have professional jobs score much higher relative to other students in the American study than in the Korean study. More detail is provided in Table A.5.

Table A.4. **Australia: Demographic summary for financial literacy quintiles**

Demographic category	Levels 1-2 (lowest literacy) (%)	Levels 3-4 (%)	Levels 5-6 (%)	Levels 7-8 (%)	Levels 9-10 (highest literacy) (%)	Total (%)
Female	24	22	21	18	15	100
Male	15	18	20	22	25	100
Less than Year 10	42	19	20	11	8	100
Tertiary Degree	8	16	20	24	32	100
Looking for work	32	18	21	18	12	100
Unskilled	40	21	21	12	7	100
Professional	5	14	15	24	41	100
Single living alone	26	21	19	16	17	100
Single parent	26	24	23	14	13	100
Couple – no children	14	16	20	22	27	100
Aged 18-24	31	20	22	16	10	100
Aged 45-59	13	19	20	22	27	100
Aged 70 or over	31	23	19	13	14	100
Ave. gross annual household income	$38 600	$52 170	$55 300	$63 870	$78 180	–
Ave. savings (including super but excluding value of home)	$46 240	$88 280	$100 400	$136 300	$243 530	–

Source: ANZ Banking Group (2003), ANZ Survey of Adult Financial Literacy in Australia, www.anz.com/aus/aboutanz/Community/Programs/FinLitResearch.asp.

Respondents often feel they know more about financial matters than is actually the case

Another finding of these surveys is that consumers often think they know more about financial issues than they really do. Respondents in the United States, the United Kingdom, and Australia feel confident in their knowledge of financial issues even though when given a test on basic finance it is clear they have only a limited understanding of these issues. If they do not realise they need information, they will not be in a position to seek it.

The 2000 JumpStart survey in the United States asks students how confident they feel about their ability to manage their own finances. Sixty-five per cent of students say that they are somewhat sure or very sure of their ability to manage their own finances. However, the scores of these students are not much higher than those of their less confident peers. In Korea, the average score of the most confident students is not much higher than that of the least confident. These finding suggest that students are unable to fully judge how capable they are to manage their money. This unsupported confidence may result in reduced demand for money management courses.

Table A.5. **Results by background**

	Korea (2003)		United States (2000)	
	% of students	Mean score	% of students	Mean score
A. Parents' income				
Less than $20 000 (1.5 million wons)	9.2	40.6	12.9	46.3
$20 000 to $39 999 (1.5-3.0 million wons)	32.5	46.6	21.9	52.0
$40 000 to $79 999 (3.0-4.5 million wons)	17.5	46.9	27.8	57.2
$80 000 or more (4.5 million wons +)	14.3	46.3	14.7	55.0
Don't know	26.0	43.5	21.6	46.5
B. Highest level of parents' education				
Neither finished H.S.	5.5	39.7	12.7	47.0
Completed H.S.	40.8	44.7	24.4	49.7
Some college	7.4	44.5	24.8	53.8
College grad or more	38.7	47.3	32.0	55.1
Don't know	7.1	42.0	5.6	45.5
C. Educational plans				
No further education	3.4	32.7	1.7	39.7
2-year of Jr. college	4.2	37.3	16.3	47.3
4-year college	78.4	47.0	68.5	54.5
Other training or ed.	6.1	39.1	8.0	46.3
Don't know	7.3	40.9	5.2	44.1
D. Planned occupation				
Manual work	2.3	30.3	3.9	38.7
Skilled trade	5.5	40.6	5.5	43.6
Service worker	11.1	41.8	9.8	41.3
Office worker	14.4	43.9	–	–
Professional worker	50.5	46.7	61.6	55.0
Other/don't know	15.3	44.6	18.6	49.0
E. Expected full-time income				
Under $15 000 (0.5 million wons)	1.9	34.9	3.6	40.6
$15 000 to $19 999 (0.5-1.0 million wons)	13.2	46.3	7.4	41.7
$20 000 to $29 999 (1.0-2.0 million wons)	47.4	47.6	21.8	53.4
$30 000 or more (2.0 million wons +)	29.3	24.3	51.2	54.4
Don't know	7.4	43.6	15.1	49.0

Source: Korea – Response to OECD questionnaire on financial education, July 2003. United States – L. Mandell (2001), *Improving Financial Literacy: What Schools and Parents Can and Cannot Do*, The Jumpstart Coalition for Personal Financial Literacy, Washington D.C.

Box A.2. **Financial Literacy in the United States – Demographic Differences**

In the Louis Harris poll of 1999 for the National Council on Economic Education, college graduate adults have significantly higher scores than non-college graduates. White adults score higher than black or Hispanic adults. With respect to students, 12th graders score higher than students in lower grades. Students who have taken an economics course score higher. Students who have college educated parents score higher, as do students who usually receive A's (NCEE, 1999).

Table A.6. **Results by perceived knowledge**

Money management knowledge compared to others

	Korea (2003)		United States (2000)	
	% of students	Mean score	% of students	Mean score
Above average	16.4	45.6	33.1	53.4
Average	39.8	47.0	49.3	52.3
Below average	17.9	43.2	9.9	49.7
Don't know	25.0	43.9	6.9	46.0

Source: Korea – Response to OECD questionnaire on financial education, July 2003. United States – L. Mandell (2001), *Improving Financial Literacy: What Schools and Parents Can and Cannot Do*, The Jumpstart Coalition for Personal Financial Literacy, Washington D.C.

This disconnect between perception and actual understanding is also noted in the surveys conducted in the United Kingdom and in Australia. The British survey finds that there is a sometimes large difference between respondents' perceptions of reality and that reality itself. For example, respondents to the survey state that they have all the information they need to make the right choice of financial product. However, during the course of the qualitative research prior to the survey, individuals brought up a number of problems with financial information: not knowing what products are available or appropriate for their needs, being overwhelmed and confused by information in leaflets, not understanding the jargon and terminology in the information and advice received, being shocked, surprised or disillusioned by the small print for financial products they had taken out, and being unaware of how to access comparative information on products. These differing perceptions suggest that the way in which questions are asked is very important in order to get the right information. For example, only seven per cent of the respondents to the survey in the United Kingdom identified financial information and advice as something that might help them to make financial plans in the future.

In the case of Australia, the results initially appear quite positive. The survey finds that 97 per cent of respondents have an ordinary banking account, 80 per cent feel "well informed" when making financial decisions, and 90 per cent feel they know how to use automated teller machines (ATMs), checks, and credit cards. In addition, at least 89 per cent appear to understand the importance of prioritising needs in order to balance income and expenditure, the basics of superannuation, the importance of making honest and complete disclosure of their circumstances, and the importance of personal identification number (PIN) security and the implications of breaching it.

However, it is one thing to feel that one understands an issue when it is presented and another to apply that understanding to a real-life problem. The Australian survey comes up with some interesting results when it compares answers to questions that ask about perceptions with those to questions that test abilities. When asked their perceptions, respondents state they are financially literate. However, when asked to apply their financial knowledge to solve a particular problem, they demonstrate a lack of financial understanding. Sixty-seven per cent of respondents, for example, indicate that they understand the term "compound interest". However, when asked to solve a problem using the concept of compound interest, only 28 per cent have a "good" level of understanding. Eighty-five per cent of respondents feel they can read and understand records relating to bank accounts, ATMS, credit cards and store cards. Yet, 25 per cent have difficulty with a practical example in which respondents are asked to read a bank statement accurately and add three numbers. Although 85 per cent of Australians know that high returns mean high risk, 47 per cent when presented with an investment advertised as having a high return but no risk would have made some level of investment.

Consumers feel financial information is difficult to find and understand

The surveys that use a subjective measure of financial literacy all note that many consumers find financial information hard to locate and difficult to understand. The Japanese Consumer Survey on Finance finds that respondents feel frustrated about the difficulty of finding easy to understand information on financial products. When asked about the financial information provided by various organisations and companies, 39 per cent of respondents say they have not seen much information, 29 per cent find the content of the information rather difficult and hard to follow, 27 per cent have the impression that a lot of the information is actually written in the interest of financial institutions, and only 5 per cent find the information provided by these organisations through brochures and on the Internet useful enough to gain knowledge about financial products and the operation of the economy and financial markets. Fifty per cent say they do not actively seek information on finance because of the impression

Box A.3. **Australia: Examples of subjective and objective questions and the different conclusions about Financial Literacy**

Understanding compound interest

Subjective question

Do you understand the term "compound interest" very well, fairly well, not very well or not at all?

67% of respondents state that they understand very well or fairly well.

Objective question

Suppose you have $1 000 to invest. Bank A offers to pay you 10% simple interest on your $1 000. Bank B offers to pay you 10% compound interest on your $1 000. Please circle as many of the statements below that appear to be true.

	% responding
a) Bank A will calculate interest that is based on the initial principal and accumulated interest	11
b) Bank B will calculate interest that is based on the initial principal and accumulated interest	68
c) The difference between the income earned with Bank A compared with the income earned with Bank B will become larger over time	45
d) If investing your money with Bank B, you would prefer compounding to occur weekly instead of monthly	54
e) Don't know	14

Comment

Consistent with the findings of the question above, 68% understand the basic concept of compound interest, that interest is earned on interest. However, only 28% of respondents selected all of *b*, *c*, and *d* as the correct response to this question and, therefore, would be described as having a "good" understanding of this concept. This example illustrates why the determination of the level of financial literacy should not be based on questions that ask individuals to self assess their level of financial understanding. The self-assessment if often higher than the actual understanding.

Box A.3. **Australia: Examples of subjective and objective questions and the different conclusions about Financial Literacy** *(cont.)*

Ability to read and understand financial records

Subjective question

Do you receive (financial records for particular payment method or financial product/service)? Do you read these at all? And how well do you understand them?

	% of users receiving records, and reading and understanding them very well or fairly well
Superannuation	60
Other investments	59
Insurance	71
Loans, other than mortgage	72
Bank accounts	89
ATMs	86
Credit cards or store cards	91

Objective question

Respondents are given a sample bank statement which lists 8 different debits, all including a transaction description and the amount of the debit. They are then asked to calculate the total amount withdrawn from ATMs. This requires identifying the three withdrawals from ATMs and adding them up. Twenty-five per cent of respondents are not able to calculate the correct amount.

Comment

Although 89% of respondents state that they have a good understanding of bank statements, 25% of respondents are not able to correctly identify the ATM withdrawals on a typical statement and add them up correctly. This is another example of self-assessments of financial understanding that are higher than the actual level of understanding.

Understanding risk

Subjective question

An investment with a high return is likely to have higher than average risk. True or false?

85% of respondents answered true.

Box A.3. **Australia: Examples of subjective and objective questions and the different conclusions about Financial Literacy** (*cont.*)

Objective question

Which ONE of the following would you recommend for an investment advertised as having a return well above market rates and no risk? (Asked of respondents with investments or insurance.)

	%
Consider it "to good to be true" and not invest	46
Invest lightly to see how it goes before investing more heavily	44
Invest heavily to maximise your return	3
Can't answer	7

Comment

This example illustrates the difference between knowing about a concept, on the one hand, and truly understanding it and applying it to one's own financial decisions. This example also illustrates the importance of basing an assessment of financial literacy on responses to questions that require the application of financial knowledge to particular applications and situations as opposed to asking for an individual's self-assessment of his/her own financial understanding.

Source: ANZ Banking Group (2003), *ANZ Survey of Adult Financial Literacy in Australia,* www.anz.com/aus/aboutanz/Community/Programs/FinLitResearch.asp.

that finance is a complicated subject. Thirty-five per cent say there is not enough accurate easy-to-understand information available on financial products. Thirty-one per cent say they do not know how to obtain accurate information on finance. Twenty-eight per cent say that even though they gather information, a lot of it is hard to understand. And 34 per cent say they can get along without any financial knowledge.

In the British survey, lack of money is not the only reason given by people who have not purchased or considered purchasing financial products in the last five years. They also cite a lack of knowledge of finance and financial products and the perceived complexity of financial products. The British survey finds that respondents spend very little time shopping around to get the best deal on financial products. The reasons given are that consumers feel overwhelmed and confused by all the information that is available and that they do not know how to access comparative information. This survey also finds that consumers do not actively seek out financial information. The information they receive, they obtain by luck, by chance, or by accident, for example, by picking up a pamphlet at a bank or having a chance talk with someone at the bank. According to the survey, about half of the respondents do some shopping around, about a fifth look at a lot of companies and about a third look at a few companies. One quarter just go to one company and a fifth rely on family and friends. Almost a third of those using an adviser rely entirely on the adviser and do not do their own research.

Consumers obtain financial information in a variety of ways

In the Japanese Survey on Consumer Finance, when consumers are asked about their main sources of information and knowledge about financial issues, 65 per cent cite TV programmes, newspapers and magazine articles, and another 37 per cent mention advertisements on TV and in newspapers and magazines. Thirty-six per cent of respondents say they get their information from product brochures of financial institutions and 34 per cent mention explanations by financial institutions' counter staff and sales people. Thirty-three per cent mention conversations with family and friends, 10 per cent mention books, and 6 per cent mention the Internet. Two per cent mention pamphlets and seminars of organisations not connected to any particular industry and one per cent mention schools. (These low percentages for the last three could be due to fact that, for example, there are not many lessons or lectures offered in schools. The question does not ask how they prefer to receive information, but rather how they actually receive it. This could be a supply problem rather than a demand problem.)

The British survey also finds that consumers obtain information on financial topics from a variety of sources. However, the ranking of the sources of financial information is different for the British respondents than for the Japanese. Thirty-nine per cent of respondents get their financial information from face-to-face contact, 27 per cent through leaflet or brochure, 18 per cent through newspaper articles, 17 per cent from talking to family and friends, and 10 per cent through advertisements. Public meetings and speakers for community groups appeal least to respondents. An added benefit of this survey is its ability to relate type of medium preferred to demographic characteristics. Lower income groups favour consumer helplines. Lower income groups and the unemployed also prefer to receive information through TV and radio programmes. The higher income and skill groups are most likely to read newspaper financial pages. Web sites appeal most to younger respondents and to the upper income groups. Younger age groups are also more likely to rely on family and friends and to use leaflets and booklets. Independent advisors are least used by those at lower socio-economic levels, the young, and the unemployed.

Notes

1. The Jumpstart Coalition for Personal Financial Literacy was founded in 1995 to evaluate the financial literacy of young adults, develop and disseminate standards of financial literacy, and promote the teaching of personal finance. Its board of directors and its partners represent a cross-section of the corporate and non-profit sectors (*www.jumpstart.org*).

2. Selected questions from the Jumpstart Financial Literacy Survey are given in Appendix A.3.

3. No information is currently available on the methodology used in the Korean survey.

4. Selected questions from this survey are given in Appendix A.1.

5. Response to OECD's questionnaire on financial education sent to delegates of the Committee on Financial Markets. Selected questions from this survey are given in Appendix A.2.

6. Bank deposits are protected up to 10 million yen in deposit principal, plus interest income, on a per-financial institution and a per-depositor basis.

7. The survey concludes that most Australians have a "reasonable" level of financial literacy. However, many of the questions used to determine this financial literacy level are ones that asked respondents to rate their own level of financial understanding. Individuals often think they know more about financial issues than is actually the case. Consequently, a determination of financial literacy based on self-assessment questions is likely to have an upward bias. This suggests that the level of financial literacy in Australia may be less than that calculated by the recent survey.

References

ANZ Banking Group (2003), *ANZ Survey of Adult Financial Literacy in Australia*, *www.anz.com/aus/aboutanz/Community/Programs/FinLitResearch.asp*, accessed 21 October 2004.

Central Council for Financial Services Information (2002), *Public Opinion Survey on Household Financial Assets and Liabilities*, *www.saveinfo.or.jp/e*, accessed 21 June 2004.

Financial Services Authority (FSA) (2000), "Better Informed Consumers", *Consumer Research Document #1*, *www.fsa.gov.uk/pubs/consumer-research/crpr01.pdf*, accessed 18 August 2003.

German Embassy Online (2003), "Survey Finds Germans Lack Investment Savvy", *The Week in Germany: Economics and Technology*, 6 June, *www.germany-info.org*, accessed 17 February 2004.

Mandell, L. (2001), *Improving Financial Literacy: What Schools and Parents Can and Cannot Do*, The Jumpstart Coalition for Personal Financial Literacy, Washington D.C., *www.jumpstart.org/pdf/financialliteracybook.pdf*, accessed 29 September 2003.

Mandell, L. (2004), 2004 Personal Finance Survey of High School Seniors, executive summary, The Jumpstart Coalition for Personal Financial Literacy, Washington D.C.,*www.jumpstart.org/download.cfm*, accessed 3 November 2004.

National Council on Economic Education (NCEE) (1999), *NCEE Standards in Economics: Survey of Students and the Public*, *www.ncee.net/cel/results.php*, accessed 3 November 2004.

APPENDIX A.1

Australia: Selected Questions from the Financial Literacy Survey

Questions about financial understanding

1. There are various ways of paying for goods and services. Which of the following payment methods do you use: ATMs, checks, credit cards, laybys, money orders, loans, store cards, telephone banking, debit cards, Internet banking.

2. Are you aware that there are Internet sites which provide calculators for comparing interest rates and overall costs of financial products? Have you visited an Internet site with calculators? Did you use the calculators to compare interest rates and overall costs of financial products?

	%
Aware of, visited, and used calculators	19
Aware of, visited but didn't use calculators	5
Aware of but haven't visited	34
Not aware of	41

Questions about financial competence

3. Which of the following do you have yourself or jointly with someone else: account with bank or credit union, vehicle insurance, house insurance, superannuation, private health insurance, life insurance, mortgage, investments other than superannuation, shares, term deposits, personal loan, investment property, loan by line of credit or overdraft, lease or hire purchase agreement, mortgage on investment property, home equity loan, margin loan.

4. For the financial products or services that you use, please indicate how well you know about the fees and charges that apply, during both take-up and during subsequent use: very well, fairly well, not very well or not at all well.

	Using	Using and knowing very well or fairly well
Superannuation	71	31
Telephone banking	36	20
Shares	44	25
Other investments	29	17
Internet banking	28	19
Debit cards	34	26
Term deposits	24	18
Store cards	15	11
Non-mortgage loans	47	36
Bank accounts	97	76
ATMs	73	60
Mortgages	38	31
Credit cards	64	56

5. Which of the following is most important when arranging superannuation or an investment? (asked of adults with superannuation or investments).

	%
The amount of return left after the fees are taken out	59
The return	14
The fees	6
Can't say	18
The per-unit cost	2

6. When arranging a new (particular financial product/service), do you hop around a lot, a fair bit, a little, or not at all?

	Percentage of all adults	
	Using	Using and shopping around a lot or a fair bit
Financial specialist	51	12
Superannuation	71	16
Ordinary bank account	97	32
Non-mortgage loan	47	21
Insurance	91	46
Mortgage	38	21
Other investment	61	34

IMPROVING FINANCIAL LITERACY – ISBN 92-64-01256-7 – © OECD 2005

7. Do you receive (financial records for particular payment method or financial product/service)? Do you read them? How well do you understand them?

	Receiving and understanding very well or fairly well (%)
Superannuation	60
Other investments	59
Insurance	71
Non-mortgage loans	72
Bank accounts	89
ATMs	86
Credit cards or store cards	91

8. I have worked out how much I will need to save for my retirement. Please indicate whether you strongly agree, agree, disagree or strongly disagree with the statement.
37% of respondents strongly agree or agree.

9. How do you expect your superannuation to provide for you in retirement?

	% of those with superannuation
More comfortably than I'm living now	11
About as comfortably as I'm living now	39
Less comfortably than now but getting by OK	34
Less comfortably than now, and not coping	12
Can't say	4

10. Which ONE of the following is the most accurate statement about fluctuations in market value?

	% of those with investments or insurance
a) Short-term fluctuations in market value can be expected, even with good investments	63
b) Good investments are always increasing in value	19
c) Investments that fluctuate in value are not good in the long-term	6
d) Can't answer	13

11. How well do you understand the following terms: bank check, direct debit, under-insurance, compound interest, broker, capital guaranteed, master trust, charge-back on a credit card, guarantor, co-borrower, indicative rate, and mortgage insurance?

APPENDIX A.2

Japan: Selected Questions from the Consumer Survey on Finance

12. How much is your knowledge and understanding of financial products and the mechanisms of the economy and finance? (Choose up to three answers.)

	%
a) Can get along without any financial knowledge	34.5
b) Did not actively seek information on finance, because of the impression that finance was a complicated subject	50.1
c) Invested funds mainly in deposits and savings with principals guaranteed, and did not anticipate any bankruptcies or collapses of financial institutions	33.1
d) Do not know ho to obtain accurate information on finance	31.2
e) Not enough accurate information easy to understand available on financial products	35.4
f) Even though gathered information, a lot of it is hard to understand	28.0
g) Other	2.7

13. Please choose the description that best matches the degree of your knowledge for each item listed from (a) through (j). (Please choose one answer for each item.)

	Know well (%)	Known to some extent (%)	Have heard of it but don't know details (%)	Have not heard of it (%)
a) Pay-out or "Payoff"	8.2	24.6	37.1	29.7
b) Expected rate of return on life insurance	3.9	27.3	42.3	26.1
c) Defined contribution plan	2.3	11.8	31.1	54.0
d) Inheritance tax	11.3	62.0	23.2	3.2
e) Financial Instruments sales tax	1.8	11.3	41.3	44.7
f) Revolving payments	13.1	28.5	22.9	35.1
g) Compound interest	17.8	40.6	28.7	12.5
h) Diversified investment portfolio	3.4	12.0	27.9	56.1
i) Risk and return	9.6	25.7	33.8	56.1
j) Money supply	3.8	12.1	45.9	38.0

IMPROVING FINANCIAL LITERACY – ISBN 92-64-01256-7 – © OECD 2005

14. What are your views about the information on finance provided by various organisations and companies? (Choose one answer.)

	%
a) Useful enough to gain knowledge on financial products and the mechanisms of the economy and finance, by reading pamphlets and searching into Web sites	4.8
b) The content of information is rather difficult and hard to follow	29.3
c) Have got the impression that a lot of information is actually written in the interest of financial institutions	27.3
d) Have not seen much information	38.6

15. What type of information do you want to have? (Choose up to three answers.)

	%
a) Deposits and savings	51.3
b) Stocks	10.8
c) Bonds (public and corporate)	5.5
d) Investment trusts	7.8
e) Pensions	67.9
f) Insurance	47.4
g) Tax, such as inheritance tax	35.6
h) Loans and credit	7.8
i) Want nothing in particular	10.7

16. What are your main sources of information and knowledge on finance? (Choose up to three.)

	%
a) Explanations by financial institutions' counter staff and sales people	34.5
b) Product brochures of financial institutions	35.9
c) Books	10.2
d) TV programmes, newspaper and magazine articles (excluding advertisements)	65.0
e) Advertisements on TV, in newspapers and magazines	37.0
f) Internet surfing	5.9
g) Conversations with family members and/or friends	33.5
h) Pamphlets and seminars of organisations that are not connected to any particular industry	2.4
i) Lessons and/or lectures at schools	1.5

APPENDIX A.3

United States: Selected Questions from the JumpStart Financial Literacy Survey

Questions on understanding income

1. If you went to college and earned a 4-year degree, how much more money could you expect to earn than if you only had a high school diploma?

   a) about 10 times as much;

   b) a lot more, about 70 per cent more;

   c) a little more, about 20 per cent more;

   d) no more, I would make about the same either way.

   The correct answer is b). This question was answered correctly by 52.2 of students.

2. Which of the following best describes the primary sources of income for most people age 20-35?

   a) profits from business;

   b) dividends and interest;

   c) rents;

   d) salaries, wages, tips.

   The correct answer is d). This question was answered correctly by 71.2 per cent of students.

Questions on understanding money management

3. Inflation can cause difficulty in many ways. Which group would have the greatest problem during periods of high inflation?

   a) young couples with no children who both work;

   b) young working couples with children;

   c) older, working couples saving for retirement;

   d) older people living on fixed retirement income.

IMPROVING FINANCIAL LITERACY – ISBN 92-64-01256-7 – © OECD 2005

The correct answer is d). Only 40 per cent of students answered this question correctly.

4. If each of the following persons had the same amount of take-home pay, who would need the greatest amount of life insurance?

   a) a young, single woman without children;

   b) an elderly retired man, with a wife who is also retired;

   c) a young married man without children;

   d) a young single woman with two young children.

   The correct answer is d). Slightly more than 50 per cent of students answered this question correctly.

Questions about understanding savings and investment

5. Bob and Cindy are the same age. At age 25 Cindy began saving $2 000 a year while Bob saved nothing. At age 50, Bob realised that he needed money for retirement and started saving $4 000 per year while Cindy kept saving her $2 000. Now they are both 75 years old. Who has the most money in his or her retirement account?

   a) Bob, because he saved more each year;

   b) They would each have the same amount because they put away exactly the same;

   c) Cindy, because she has put away more money;

   d) Cindy, because her money has grown for a longer time at compound interest.

   The correct answer is d). Half the students answered this question correctly.

6. Many people put aside money to take care of unexpected expenses. If Pedro and Susanna have money put aside for emergencies, in which of the following forms would it be of LEAST benefit to them if they needed it right away?

   a) checking account;

   b) savings account;

   c) stocks;

   d) invested in a down payment on the house.

   The correct answer is d). Just under half of the students answered this question correctly.

Questions on understanding spending and debt

7. Under which of the following circumstances would it be financially beneficial to you to borrow money to buy something now and repay it with future income?

   a) when you really need a 2-week vacation;

   b) when some clothes you like go on sale;

   c) when the interest on the loan is grater than the interest you get on your savings;

   d) when you need to buy a car to get a much better paying job.

   The correct answer is d). Just 54.4 per cent of students answered this question correctly.

8. Which of the following credit card users is likely to pay the GREASTEST dollar amount in finance charges per year if they all charge the same amount per year on their cards?

   a) Barbara, who always pays off her credit card bill in full shortly after she receives it;

   b) Ellen, who generally pays off her credit card in full but occasionally will pay the minimum when she is short of cash;

   c) Nancy, who pays at least the minimum amount each month and more when she has the money;

   d) Paul, who only pays the minimum amount each month.

   The correct answer is d). Just 60.7 of students answered this question correctly.

ANNEX B

Investment/retirement Saving and Financial Education: Additional Information

Individual and social benefits of financial education

Financial education programmes can contribute to the well-being of workers in retirement by providing them with the information and skills to make wise investment choices with both their pension plans and any individual savings plans. By providing accurate, objective, and easily understandable information, such as a discussion of investment terms and descriptions of the features of different types of investments, financial education programmes can help workers select the investment products and services that are most appropriate for their individual situations. This function of financial education programmes would help allay the concerns expressed by a number of countries that consumers are confused by financial jargon. For example, research by the Irish Financial Services Regulatory Authority (IFSRA) finds that for 75 per cent of consumers the written information on financial products is too difficult to understand (Keena, 2004). The development of these skills will address concerns expressed by a number of countries that workers might not be capable of adequately saving for their retirement.

Financial education programmes can also contribute to the well-being of workers by teaching them to be wary of schemes that promise high returns with low risks and by helping them ask the right questions about financial products and services. Among the examples of risky or fraudulent investments listed in the box below are several in which consumers were advised to invest in stocks or bonds that were not financially sound. Financial education programmes might have helped protect some of the individuals involved in these investments. For example, a financially educated investor would know that he should not concentrate an entire investment portfolio in one stock, whether this is his personal savings or an employer-provided defined contribution plan.

Box B.1. **Examples of Risky or Fraudulent Investments**

Italy

The collapse of a number of important Italian companies in the past few years – such as Parmalat, Cirio – and the technical default of several others have wiped out the savings of many thousands of individual Italian investors. These individual investors began buying bonds in the late 1990s when the yields on government bonds fell. Unfortunately, these investors looked only at the high returns and badly underestimated the risk. In the case of Parmalat, both the company and the local banks encouraged workers to invest in Parmalat bonds.

United States

Senior management at Enron actively encouraged workers to invest in Enron stock even though they likely knew it was artificially priced. Many of the members of Enron's 401(k) plan had large percentages of their assets invested in Enron stock. And, unlike Enron's defined benefit scheme, the contributions to the defined contribution scheme were not protected by government-backed insurance. As a result, when Enron collapsed, many employees lost their entire retirement savings.

United Kingdom

In the late 1980s and 1990s, people were persuaded, wrongly as it runs out, to move from their occupational pensions into personal pensions. Many of these pensions were misrepresented to potential buyers. Deceptive advertising led many workers to leave plans provided by their employers or the government and move into private plans that in fact offered inferior benefits. A large percentage of these workers were women and those with the lowest incomes. In this case, it wasn't only the workers that lost money. Between 1987 and 1995, the government spent 21.7 billion pounds on insurance rebates and incentives.

Netherlands

A booming stock market in the late 1990s, accompanied in some cases by aggressive marketing, resulted in six per cent of families entering into contracts to borrow money in order to invest in stocks, A relatively large number of these families were low-income families. When the financial markets collapsed, many of these families were left with substantial debts.

Ireland

A large number of consumers who invested in the state-owned telecommunications company, Eircom, lost money as a result of the poor performance of the stock. These consumers were unaware of the risks involved. Some consumers had even borrowed in order to invest in this stock.

Financial education programmes can also help governments explain to the public the need for pension reform, typically the need to move in whole or in part from a traditional pay-as-you-go programme to a funded programme. The recent Slovak government media campaign is an example of a successful explanation of reform. In addition, in countries in which pension reform is occurring, it is very important that workers be aware of the necessity of making sound investment decisions and that they be provided with the information that will enable them to do so. Financial education programmes can explain these pension reforms to consumers and help consumers make appropriate choices. Financial education programmes can also help to inform individuals how newly established pension programmes work and of their rights and obligations under them.

To the extent that workers successfully contribute to defined contribution plans and personal savings plans as a result of financial education programmes, financial pressure is taken off government provided pay-as-you-go schemes.

Description of current investment/retirement programmes

Selected programmes

Publications

In Austria, a wide variety of investment publications are offered by private, non-profit entities such as the employees' association and consumer organisations. The employees' association, the Austrian Chamber of Labour (BAK), publishes and distributes brochures targeted at employees (such as *The Savings Book, Financial Investment and Financial Advisor, Building Loan Agreement, 10 Steps to Employee Assessment*). These brochures cover issues specific to employees and include information on all kinds of investment products in which they could potentially be interested, including stocks, securities and funds. For each particular investment product discussed, the publications also point out the associated advantages, disadvantages and risks. Published in October 2003, these brochures are also available on the Internet. Austrian consumer organisations, such as the Austrian Consumer Protection Association (VKI), issue a range of booklets offering advice on investment targeted to all investors and, which, unlike those offered by the BAK, must be purchased. These booklets focus more on the topics of general money handling and investing. Titles include: *How to invest correctly, building society savings, foreign currency loans, debit and credit cards* (2000), *A better way to invest money* (January 2001), *The practices of banks – the chances for consumers* (2002), *Practical Guidebook: Protection of investors – classes of investors and risks, guarantee and earnings.Basics for beginners on the stock exchange* (September 2003) and *Investment Funds in Comparison* (September 2004).

The Polish Securities and Exchange Commission (PSEC), a central governemtn authority, produced in 2003 the "Investor's Guide", which included basic information on investing in the Polish capital market. Updated and reissued in 2004, this guide initiated a series of brochures targeted at beginner investors (i.e. those with no dealings in the capital markets as yet and wanting to learn about investment possibilities or those who have just begun investing in the capital markets). Three Investor's Guides, entitled *Investment Funds, What to Invest In-Investments ABC*, and *Sources of Information on the Capital Market*, were published in 2004. In addition, the PSEC prepared a booklet on the Individual Compensation Scheme, which the Polish authorities consider is particularly important from the investors' point of view. The PSEC also published a series of books providing detailed information on the capital market for more financially literate investors. The Spanish National Commission of Securities Markets (CNMV) publishes Investor Information Guides on topics related to different areas of the securities market (i.e. intermediaries, products, etc.). One set of guides is published under the title *What you need to know about...*, and deals with the main securities market topics, such as mutual funds, fixed-income products, and the rights and responsibilities of shareholders. In 2003, 200 000 copies were distributed free to investors. The CNMV intends to accompany the launch of new and more sophisticated products (e.g. equities, derivative products, etc.) with a further set of *Investors' Guides*, in order to familiarise more experienced investors with more complex financial services.

Web sites

In Italy and Spain, the Web sites of the countries' respective supervisory and regulatory authorities (Consob in Italy and CNMV in Spain), both feature an *Investors' Corner* to draw the investor's attention to relevant information. Consob's *Investors' Corner* is divided into four sections: the first section, "Warnings" includes the latest notifications (from Consob or corresponding foreign authorities) about frauds or abusive activities; the second, "Dos and don'ts", gives suggestions to follow before, during and after signing an investment contract and particularly underlines the importance of an appropriate information relationship between investors and intermediaries; the third, "Know the risks", is a page stating the risks of investments in financial instruments; the fourth and final section, "Investor education" (launched in 2001) details all the educational campaigns elaborated by Consob as well as including other helpful information pages.[1] The *Investors' Corner* (*Rincón del inversor*) of CNMV's Web site gives clear, detailed information on the functioning of Spanish securities markets, and is organised in a similar way to its Italian counterpart: it is clearly divided into three sections – Information, Help to Investors and Warnings.[2] *Investors' Corners* are also found on the Web sites of the regulatory and supervisory authorities of Turkey and Japan.

Training courses

In the Czech Republic, Fit for Investment, a programme targeting private investors and initiated in 2002, is provided by EKIA (an information agency). Partners in the programme include the Association for Capital Markets (AKAT) and The Union of Investment Companies (UNIS CR). The main aims of the programme are to enhance knowledge of public investors about investment principles and to reinforce trust in the capital market. The programme does this through a series of training courses and annual conferences, called "Investment Opportunities", and the "Fond Market". The seminars attract over 300 individual investors every year in most major cities but mainly in Prague. In 2004, Fit For Investment continued to draw on the financial support of major Czech capital market players, such as IKS KB, FIO, Pioneer Investment and others.

In the United States, employer-provided financial education programmes include those operated by companies such as United Parcel Service (since 2000) and Weyerhaeuser Ltd. (since 1984) on long-term planning for savings and retirement. Both initiatives include classes of one or two days in length and are offered at regular intervals, with keen support from management. They are targeted at specific age groups and provide employee participants with a good range of resources and written materials (such as coursebook manuals which include explanations as to how company benefits fit into broader financial planning strategies). Building on existing written materials and resources, the UPS programme offers a Web-based service assisting employees with the development of a personal financial action plan as well as computer software providing advice on debt management, budgeting, insurance, and retirement and personal savings. By contrast, Weyerhaeuser Ltd. approaches its programme provision in a more "holistic" way: the company's programme covers non-financial advice for employees such as how to improve their quality of life and maintain good health (Braunstein and Welch, 2002).

Public education campaigns

In the United States, the public information campaign, *Choose to Save*, advocates the idea that in order to ensure a secure financial situation for the future, consumers must start saving today.[3] The programme, provided by the non-profit Employee Benefit Research Institute (EBRI), is delivered nationally using a wide range of media including newspapers, radio, television, and the Internet, train and bus advertisements and conferences. Partners such as the United States Department of Labor co-operate on producing written materials including booklets (*The Power to Choose*) and brochures (*Top Ten Ways To Save for Retirement*). Public service announcements originally developed for radio and television stations in just one metropolitan area are now broadcast in forty-nine states. Meanwhile, since 1997, four television news specials called *The Savings Game* have been broadcast on primetime in one metro area and also nationally on cable stations, with the total value of their airtime already exceeding $20 million. Internet tools are also provided such as the *Ballpark Estimate Retirement Planning Worksheet*, which helps consumers estimate how much they need for retirement savings, and over 100 online financial calculators, which assist investors with a wide range of financial planning issues including credit, budgeting, home purchase mortgages and all aspects of their future financial security. Funding and materials for these programmes have been provided by private sector companies, partner institutions of the American Savings Education Council (ASEC) and EBRI members.

The OECD also identified a further public financial education campaign offered in the United States. Entitled *America Saves*,[4] the campaign's main goal is to encourage and help consumers towards savings and wealth accumulation. In operation since 2001 and enrolling around 20 000 individual savers, it is co-ordinated and managed at local, state and national levels by the Consumer Federation of America (CFA), a Washington-based federation of consumer advocacy, research and education organisations. Also active in the campaign are 1 000 nonprofit groups, employers, financial institutions, consumer education, advocacy associations and government agencies whose role is to provide and promote savings services to consumers. In addition, motivational workshops, one-on-one consultations, and no-fee savings accounts are offered. The Financial Planning Association, for example, which makes its members' pro bono services available to individual savers, plays a key role in the campaign. Moreover, representatives from a variety of governmental and nonprofit organisations, such as the United States Department of Labor, the Federal Reserve Board, the American Savings and Education Council, and the National Foundation for Credit Counseling, function as national programme advisors. Where financing is concerned, the initiative's core national funder is the nonprofit Ford Foundation. Other financers include GSEs, Fannie Mae and Freddie Mac, nonprofits, (such as the Fannie Mae Foundation, the National Credit Union Foundation and InCharge Institute), and a number of companies. At local level, funding is provided by banks, credit unions, Cooperative Extension offices and community foundations. The initiative has expanded since its pilot programme started in Cleveland Ohio, with further campaigns initiated and planned in three more cities including Kansas City, Indianapolis and Charlotte (Braunstein and Welch, 2002). Since its beginnings in 2001, the campaign has attracted around 20 000 savers to enroll.

In Mexico, the 1997 reform replaced the country's pay-as-you-go (PAYG) system with a defined contribution system based on individual capitalisation accounts managed by specialised financial institutions, called the Afores. The new pension system has generated a need to provide more information for workers and to introduce them to a basic financial education scheme related to the pension system. The Mexican government agency, Consar, has responsibility for disseminating such information on the new pension system and aims to inform workers about the importance of choosing the Afore[5] with the lowest commissions and the highest returns. It does this through a permanent information campaign provided in partnership with Afores, unions, the private sector and employer associations, and targeted to workers. The campaign's main goal is to generate interest and concern among employees about preparing effectively for their retirement. The campaign uses Internet and all media channels (TV, radio, newspapers, magazines, billboards) for its principal delivery methods. More specifically it publishes printed materials, such as advertisements in newspapers and magazines, as well as posters and banners on main Web pages.[6] It also diffuses radio and television advertisements, and places posters on information stands across the country.[7] All materials are intended to develop employees' interest in their retirement, including phrases such as: "Do you prefer 15% more or less in your retirement", "Do you know how much your Afore is charging you?", "Are you indifferent?" Moreover Consar agents make personal visits to companies and associations, and seminars and round tables are also organised. As a result, Consar has succeeded in achieving a closer relationship with workers, thus allowing them to understand and acknowledge all the options they have to increase their personal savings for retirement.

Notes

1. These information pages include informational documents on "Mutual funds", offering information in plain language about these products; "Covered warrants and structured bonds", a page helping investors understand the specific features (e.g. reverse convertibilty) of these structured financial products and offering animated presentations as well as two calculators making it easier to calculate the price of structured bonds or to compare the price of similar covered warrant offered in the market.

2. Also to be found on the CNMV Web site are columns offering concrete, practical advice when dealing with investment institutions and intermediaries, warning messages on unregistered companies, a list of necessary precautions for investors in order to operate safely in the securities markets and glossaries of financial terms (available at www.mineco.es/tesoro/htm/deuda/index_en.htm).

3. More information available from: www.choosetosave.org.

4. It is accessible at www.americasaves.org/.

5. Specialised financial entities managing and promoting the individual accounts part of Mexico's system and responsible for the investment of resources through the Sociedades de Inversión Especializadas en Fondos para el Retiro (Siefores) (Investment Funds Specialised in Funds for Retirement).

6. These materials include detailed information regarding the equivalent fees (a calculation made by Consar in order to make comparable the different kind of fees that the Afores charge) and how to compare the final balances you might obtain with each Afore, either by Internet or by telephone, the "final balance calculator" (a special software programme created by the Consar that gives the workers the approximate amount of money that they could have at the end of his labour life, based on their actual age, income and the Afore that manages their funds).

7. The information stands are located at commercial centers, subway stations and some strategic points in the main streets. This booths are easy recognisable and one or more specialists are there in order to resolve any questions that workers might have. They also have a variety of materials to support and extend their explanations.

References

Braunstein, S. and C. Welch (2002), "Financial Literacy: An Overview of Practice, Research and Policy", *Federal Reserve Bulletin*, Washington D.C., *www.federalreserve.gov/pubs/ bulletin/2002/1102lead.pdf#*, accessed 22 August 2003.

Keena, C. (2004), "Use of Financial Jargon in Literature Criticized by Literacy Agency", *The Irish Times*, 18 September.

ANNEX C

Financial Education on Credit and Debt: Additional Information

Background

The components of household debt

Non-mortgage consumer credit is defined by the United States Federal Reserve Board as covering "most short- and intermediate-term credit extended to individuals, excluding loans secured by real estate".[1] A broad definition is also used in the European Union. It encompasses all different forms of consumer credit: credit card use, foreign currency loans, payday loans, consumer instalment loans (which include borrowing for education and can thus be a human capital investment), hire-purchase loans, overdraft facilities, revolving/rolling credit, financial leases, and other types of consumer credit (*e.g.* auto loans and loans for purchases of consumer durables) (EC, 2002). For mortgage credit/home loans, the definition of a mortgage as any loan using the home as collateral is used. This can include home equity loans, borrowing for owner-occupation and borrowing for investment purposes (RBA, 2003). The risky loans in this category are subprime mortgage loans and predatory mortgage lending. However it should be noted that predatory lenders can be active in both the consumer credit and mortgage loan spheres.

Trends in household debt

The degree of indebtedness can be measured by a ratio of debt or debt service payments to income. In the United States, for example, the Federal Reserve Board has constructed two types of measures to assess the extent of American household indebtedness – the quarterly household debt service ratio (DSR) and the financial obligations ratio (FOR).[2] Excess indebtedness or over-indebtedness occurs when the ratios of debt or debt service payments to income exceed certain thresholds. Borrowing against housing accounts for the majority of the household debt stock in each country, reflecting the important role played by housing in providing collateral for loans (Debelle, 2004a). For example, 2004 figures show mortgage debt accounting for around 75 per cent of total household debt in the United States and the United Kingdom (Debelle, 2004b) and for over 50 per cent of total household liabilities in Austria (2003 figures).[3] Of the rise in household debt in Austria from 2000 to 2003, foreign currency loans showed a particularly sharp increase (39 per cent) (OECD, 2000), and as of 2004, foreign currency loans as a share of total private household loans in Austria amounted to 19 per cent – several times higher than the euro area average.[4] By comparison, mortgage credit and consumer loans showed smaller increases relatively speaking, (up only 17 per cent and 3 per cent respectively).[5] The fact that individuals in Austria have increasingly taken loans in foreign currency, many of whom underestimate the foreign currency risks of such loan contracts (which are usually on a long-term basis) has particular implications for credit education in this country.

With respect to the factors contributing to rising mortgage credit, first, long-term interest rates declined to historically low levels in many OECD countries over the past decade.[6] The net effect of low mortgage rates is difficult to assess up-front, as declining mortgage interest rates should enable households to reduce their monthly payment burdens. However, other things equal, low rates also mean that households are capable of taking out larger loans for a given level of household income.[7] The availability of low financing costs enables first-time buyers to purchase more expensive housing than might otherwise be feasible and allows existing homeowners to trade up to larger or more expensive homes as well. This process helps sustain the demand for housing and supports rising house prices. Rising prices are no doubt supported as well by demand from investors. Indeed, in most of the target countries, the interaction of these various factors has resulted in a steady upward trend in house prices (in the United Kingdom and the United States since the mid 1990s, and in Korea from 2001 to 2003 (OECD, 2004a), but not in Austria (ANB, 2003a). Rising house prices have also helped to support consumer spending in many countries, as various innovations over the years have enabled homeowners to more easily extract the equity that has accumulated in their homes. Thus, even in the face of relative stagnation in wages, homeowners can sustain their consumption through borrowing against home equity. Record issuance of securities backed by home equity loans suggest that homeowners have in fact been quite active in extracting home equity.[8] In some jurisdictions, deregulation in the mortgage market, in particular the relaxing of constraints on mortgage lending rates and loan to value (LTV) ratios has proved to be another significant factor behind the increase in mortgage borrowing (Debelle, 2004a). These reforms have facilitated access to the market by borrowers who would otherwise be unable to purchase homes by enabling them to qualify for loans with low down payments.

130

Credit cards have become popular over the past three decades among consumers as a fast, convenient payment tool for purchasing goods and services (and for other types of transactions). Heavy marketing and developments in technology and telecommunications also play an important part in their growing popularity (CFA, 2000). With credit card use fast expanding, the share of credit card debt in total household debt (though relatively small to date) is likely to increase in the future, making it an issue of growing concern in many countries (OECD, 2004b; Durkin, 2000; NEFE, 2002). Moreover, unlike housing loans which are backed up by equity investments, credit card debt is perhaps more worrying due to the fact that no equity investment is made and thus no assets are built up by the consumer.

In addition to banks, a number of non-bank companies now offer credit cards directly to consumers. Credit users in OECD countries find themselves presented with many new and sophisticated options for loans, credit cards, and other forms of debt. Advances in data storage and retrieval enable service providers to develop products specially targeted to specific categories of consumers. This development has been supported by improved credit-scoring techniques, which have reduced creditors' costs and contributed to a rise in the number of consumers eligible for credit. What is not always clear even to mainstream credit consumers is that the kinds of consumer protection associated with each credit product can be very different. Such complexity in the credit market is evident in the special offers targeting consumers, which sometimes prove to be more advantageous to providers. Many products (marketed as "low" interest credit cards, payment holidays on loan agreements, and interest free deals) do not in reality match up to their marketing promises and, in their small print, can present "hidden traps" for consumers.In the United Kingdom, for example, there is a particular problem with storecard debt and the cards have recently been the focus of particular public concerns.[9] These popular retailer credit cards – numbering 20 million in the United Kingdom in 2000 – often charge an annual interest rate exceeding those of traditional credit cards (sometimes over 30 per cent) (Mintel, 2001, cited CAB, 2001; CAB, 2001). An overdraft, loan, or credit card facility with a lower interest rate is available for most storecard clients, making it unadvisable for them to take out extra loans on these high interest cards (CAB, 2001).

Concern about the impact and reach of Alternative Financial Service (AFS) credit lenders and their products has been a source of public debate since the late 1990s, when news of dishonest and unjust home equity lending practices first began to emerge (Braunstein and Welch, 2002). A growing number of subprime lenders[10] now operate and predatory lending (or "extortionate" lending as it is known in the United Kingdom) is increasingly prevalent. Rollovers in payday loans also cause harm to consumers, particularly in the United Kingdom and the United States (Stegman, 2003). The terms of these loans are often ill-adapted and misleading, particularly for those with poor financial knowledge or low earnings. This problem is compounded by the fact that a large proportion of the population is not eligible for mainstream credit and is thus forced to resort to AFS for borrowing arrangements; for example, as many as a quarter of United Kingdom households are denied access to mainstream credit (NEF, 2004).

With respect to over-indebtedness and its consequences, although an alarming increase in the rate of delinquencies and personal bankruptcies is manifest across all four countries, nowhere is this crisis more acute than in the United States, where in 2003, 1.6 million households (around 9 per cent of all American households) filed for personal bankruptcy (Marcuss, 2004). The three other countries, by contrast, have far less serious delinquency and personal bankruptcy rates: in England and Wales in 2004, there were 46 650 individual insolvencies (UKDTI, 2005)[11] (around 0.09 per cent of the population) (NSUK, 2005). In Austria, during the first three quarters of 2003, there was a rise in private bankruptcies of 11.1 per cent (3 175 cases), compared to the corresponding period of 2002 (ANB, 2003b). Finally, in Korea, individual delinquent borrowers totalled 3.8 million (or 3.2 per cent) of the working-age population as of January 2004 (OECD, 2004a).

Groups most affected by debt and personal reasons for over-indebtedness

The over-indebtedness of young consumers is of special concern to policymakers, particularly in relation to credit card misuse. Recent years have seen a growing number of cases of young adults running up large credit card debts, and becoming over-indebted and credit delinquent. In Korea, for instance, a recent excessive use of credit cards by the young has led to a significant increase in the number of young individuals with bad credit.[12] Young American consumers are also finding it difficult to manage debt (of which a large proportion is credit card related): this is illustrated by figures showing that, between 1991 and 1999, bankruptcy filings have risen 51 per cent among debtors below the age of twenty-five (Braunstein and Welch, 2002). One reason why young people (as opposed to older adults) are particularly prone to running up excess credit card debts is that they are more likely than older individuals to lack the knowledge and money skills essential for managing their borrowing effectively.[13]

IMPROVING FINANCIAL LITERACY – ISBN 92-64-01256-7 – © OECD 2005

Box C.1. **In Korea, debt increasingly affects older consumers**

With respect to general credit and debt, it would seem that, in Korea, older consumers are also affected. The number of older consumers in debt has been rising: the number of credit delinquents in their 40s and older had climbed to the highest level in seven months in October 2004.* Moreover, during the fourth quarter of 2004, the ratio of credit defaulters aged 40 or over to the total number of credit defaulters blacklisted by the Korea Federation of Banks was over 50 per cent (Yon-Se, 2004). Many older Korean people are unaware of the existence of debt rescheduling programmes as a means of avoiding blacklisting, highlighting a need for financial education to make older debtors more aware of such programmes.

* Totalling 1.85 million, a rise of 7 185 from the previous month (Yon-Se, 2004).

The importance of resolving over-indebtedness and the benefits of financial education

Individual and economic consequences of over-indebtedness

Consequences for individuals

Although individuals and households can benefit greatly from borrowing, in that it provides a chance for them to finance housing, education, and durable goods, when their debt exceeds a certain amount of their income, they are left highly vulnerable to fluctuations in interest rates and changes in disposable income, so much so that if interest rates rise or if disposable incomes fall, they find themselves in severe financial distress (Debelle, 2004a; Debelle 2004b). If households with their current income at fixed levels are not capable of dealing with debt repayments, and moreover, if additional borrowings are unavailable to them, they can become credit delinquent. Once they enter delinquency, they face penalties such as high arrearage charges and limited access to regular financial transactions, as well as having the extra burden of continuing responsibility for paying off debts. At this stage, they could well be forced to file for personal bankruptcy. In such cases, it is only after these consumers have completely resolved their debt problems that they will be able to resume the kinds of lifestyles they led prior to over-indebtedness (Marcuss, 2004).

Economic consequences

With respect to the negative impact of over-indebtedness on the economy, in general, rising household borrowings cause current consumption expenditure levels to rise at first, but cause future consumption expenditure levels to decline. This is because in the initial stage of borrowing, households are able to spend more on consumption on account of the loans they take out, but, in the over-indebtedness stage, households can no longer increase their borrowing levels and have to spend some portion of household income to pay off the debt they have accumulated and/or the interest on the loan. The general excess indebtedness may be a factor contributing to the general decline in savings rates: about two decades ago (in 1984), Americans managed to save 8.8 per cent of after-tax income. By contrast the 1996 United States savings rate was just 4.9 per cent (Christenbury and Porter, 1999).

Financial education as a solution: benefits of credit and debt education and examples of how it can help the over-indebted with respect to the main points outlined above

Benefits of credit and debt education

- To consumers

OECD countries, then, face the following challenges related to consumer use of the lending market: an increase in household debt; an expansion and growing complexity of credit products; and a rise in subprime and predatory lending practices (as a respective cause and consequence of the former development). Consumers often tend to take out loans with terms that they do not understand and agree to products that are too expensive for them, making them subject to hidden costs and overcharges. Moreover, they tend to lack the confidence required to challenge the clever promotional techniques applied by credit salesmen (CAB, 2001). Behaviours such as over-commitment to credit arrangements and/or mismanagement of personal finances leave consumers vulnerable to any unexpected developments in their individual circumstances that might cause a drop in income (UKDTI and UKDWP, 2004). Excess household indebtedness is caused by one or a combination of these many factors.

These challenges clearly raise a need for debt education. While, in the past, households might have needed just a simple knowledge of bank accounts and savings, today's households require more sophisticated/ complex financial knowledge and skills about the lending industry. Without a certain level of financial literacy, the least educated and, in particular, those with poor credit histories are left vulnerable to unscrupulous lenders, to abusive lending practices, and to risks of acquiring unnecessary or inappropriate credit products. Financial education and financial literacy training supplying all consumers (and, above all, vulnerable borrowers) with information about banking, personal finance, and credit, and helping them to manage their finances more effectively can protect them against against fraud and abuse. It can thus be an effective contribution to preventing future over-indebtedness.

Box C.2. **The rationale for credit education**

- Three-fifths of United States households in 1998 claimed that they had expenditures higher than their income (Federal Reserve Board, 1998, cited Hopley, 2003). Six years later, in July 2004, outstanding United States consumer and mortgage debt stood at an estimated $9.7 trillion (8.37 per cent of GDP) and outstanding non-mortgage consumer debt was more than $2.0 trillion, after having risen 7.1 per cent annually since 1999 (Mavrinac and Ping, 2004). As clear evidence in the case for financial education, a study by Jinkook and Hogarth (1999, cited in Mavrinac and Ping 2004) suggests that consumers who comprehend credit terms better can, in general, make considerable reductions in their annual interest rate charges.

- In the United States, credit card debt levels per household are also rising dramatically on average. In 1990, typical levels of credit card debt were an average $2 985; by 2002, the figure had nearly trebled totalling $8 562. Interest rates on this debt were an annual 14.71 per cent on average (Mavrinac and Ping, 2004). In 2002, the average debt per American household owning a minimum of one credit card was $8 940 (Weston, 2005). Meanwhile, two years later, in 2004, 60 per cent of credit card owners were rolling over at least a share of their debt, while 48 per cent were paying merely the minimum required monthly instalment[*] and the average balance maintained was more than $4 000 (NEFE, 2002).

- Between 1990 and 2000, the personal bankruptcy rate in the United States rose 69 per cent and, with more than 1 million Americans filing for bankruptcy every year of that decade, bankruptcy filings, businesses included, grew 90.6 per cent (Mavrinac and Ping, 2004) (Hopley, 2003). Over 1.6 million personal bankruptcies were filed in the United States by the end of 2003, the equivalent of an estimated 2.1 million people. These filers typically owed a sum in excess of one and a half times their annual household income (Mavrinac and Ping, 2004).

- In the United States, in 2002, over 75 per cent of college undergraduate students had credit cards (most had several cards with an average total balance of $2 748) and 95 per cent of college graduate students had credit cards (four each on average with a total balance of $4 776 on average) (NEFE, 2002). Meanwhile, among the under 25s, bankruptcies have risen more than 50 per cent in the past few years, with this age group filing nearly 150 000 bankruptcies in 2000 – ten times 1995 figures (Mavrinac and Ping, 2004).

[*] According to evidence presented at a recent United States Senate hearing (Mavrinac and Ping, 2004).

• To financial institutions

This determination is not meant to suggest that it is consumers alone who stand to benefit from credit education initiatives. Financial institutions can also benefit from providing financial education programmes, and there are good reasons for why they should be encouraged to participate voluntarily in such provision. First, credit education can lead to good business for the institutions (Hawke, 2002; Willis, 2004). The process of offering and sponsoring credit education programmes enables such institutions to make contacts with potential new clients and, thus, eventually to expand their customer base (Burhouse, 2004). Second, providing such programmes would give financial institutions an opportunity to enhance their ethical and corporate social responsibility ratings: successful credit education programmes allow them to make good impressions both on programme participants (such as high school and college students) and on the wider community at large, thus enhancing their community reputations. Third, this good reputation, in turn, would give institutions an enhanced competitive edge over rival institutions – a particularly important advantage given today's climate of competition in the financial services sector. Fourth, by reducing the risks of delinquencies and personal bankruptcies, financial institutions would benefit directly from the results of these credit education programmes particularly considering, for example, that a large share of the United States' 1.6 million bankruptcies in 2003 resulted in losses for financial institutions (Marcuss, 2004). Financial consumers with good financial knowledge and skills would be less likely to file for personal bankruptcy than those without such knowledge and skills. Hence, the benefits reaped from credit education can be a real incentive for financial institutions to sponsor or participate in such programmes. Finally, it should also be recognised that the voluntary participation of financial institutions in financial education is essential for encouraging private sector-offered credit education to prosper. Thus, it is important to create incentives for financial institutions to participate in credit education easily and voluntarily.[14]

Description of financial education programmes on credit and debt[15]

The responses to the OECD's surveys show that the important role played by credit and debt education has been widely recognised by governments, financial institutions, and non-profit organisations in the four OECD countries covered in this chapter. As a result, and in response to the growing concerns about rising consumer over-indebtedness, these stakeholders in both public and private sectors – over the past decade in the United States and the United Kingdom and, more recently, in Austria and Korea[16] – have invested considerable efforts in developing and implementing appropriate programmes. Most programmes were initiated in the second half of the 1990s, although the timing and extent of their development varies across countries: the United Kingdom and the United States, for example, have a relatively long history of credit and debt education provision while, in Korea, credit and debt education has only been introduced more recently. Of all providers, non-profit organisations[17] have played a key role in providing credit and debt education. They have offered well-organised programmes and developed many effective training methods. In addition, financial institutions have also taken part in providing credit and debt education programmes in co-operation with non-profit organisations. More recently, policymakers and governments have begun to work on the provision of effective credit and debt education to all who need it. Credit and debt management has thus become a core component of public policy on financial education.

Selected examples of programmes

Below is a selection of credit education programmes, spanning both consumer loans and mortgage credit. This list is not exhaustive, but aims to provide descriptions of representative programmes that tackle consumer indebtedness. Where possible, it has also been indicated whether programmes offer "preventive" advice (educating people about how to avoid getting into debt and not get caught in the debt trap) or "curative" advice (finding solutions in the case of over-indebtedness) or, as for some cases, a combination of both.

Publications

Most credit education is offered through publications and brochures. In the United Kingdom, the Council of Mortgage Lenders (a professional association representing mortgage lending institutions) offers a range of preventive and curative brochures and fact sheets to help prospective and existing homeowners with their most common enquiries on mortgage credit and debt.[18] Five brochures and/or fact sheets, in particular, focus on arrears repossession and mortgage complaints: Assistance with Mortgage Repayments gives details of government benefits and lists agencies offering expert advice on mortgage repayments. Debt Following Mortgage Possession describes how a borrower's mortgage loan is affected after home repossession; it also discusses "shortfall debt" (when house sale proceeds are insufficient to pay off money owed to the lender) and the time limit lenders have in which to seek recovery of debt from borrowers following repossession. Mortgage Indemnity: A Borrowers Guide explains mortgage indemnity. The Possession Register gives an overview of the Register and the credit reference agencies operating it, of its aims and activities, of its information on possessions and on the borrowers and lenders affected by these possessions. Mortgage Complaints explains the action to take if a homebuyer/owner has a mortgage complaint.

In Austria, Bank Austria, a financial institution, published a preventive consumer loan brochure in 1996, Borrowing Money (Geld Borgen), in cooperation with the Association for Consumer Information (VKI). The booklet explains the fundamentals of loans and is distributed through branch banks to all credit consumers, and given out free to college and university students. The project is the first consumer-oriented book of its kind in Austria to provide all the basics on loans and financing. Similar initiatives in Austria are provided by the Chambers of Labour (professional organisations), nonprofits and consumer protection associations.

In Canada, the Consumer Education and Public Affairs Branch of the federal consumer information and protection agency, the Financial Consumer Agency of Canada, publishes a user-friendly consumer education and information kit called Credit Cards and You (FCAC, 2003-04a).[19] The kit comprises four booklets including Getting the Most from Your Credit Card:Understanding the Terms and Conditions which aims, among other objectives, to help consumers choose a credit card in accordance with their needs, to determine whether the period without interest applies to them, to take advantage of newly launched low interest rates, and save money when using the card; Playing it Safe: How to Protect Your Credit Card and Credit History, which aims to help consumers understand their credit history, to protect themselves against non-authorised transactions on their credit cards and to take action should they find non-authorised transactions on their bank statements; Your Rights and Responsibilities: The Cost of Borrowing with a Credit Card, which gives consumers information on their rights and responsibilities when shopping for a new credit card, when they receive their new card or bank statement or when their credit card contract is modified; and Managing Your Money: How to Save with a Credit Card, which provides, among other information, details on saving money by conducting payments early between bank statements, for example (FCAC, 2003-04b). Originally issued as a publication in the years 2003-04, Credit Cards and You was redesigned as a kit in January 2004 to include an interactive worksheet for use by consumers when choosing a credit card, ten tables describing different types of credit cards (such as standard and low-rate, student cards and secured cards), and a useful glossary of credit card terms.

Advisory services

Nonprofit advisory services (mainly in the form of telephone helplines) are a particularly popular delivery method for curative debt advice. One example, targeted to underserved and financially illiterate consumers, is National Debtline,[20] a British-based free telephone helpline/consumer hotline service provided by a nonprofit (registered charity) of the same name and co-ordinated by the Money Advice Trust.[21] The service offers free, confidential expert and independent curative advice supported by written self-help materials. It can also offer assistance in setting up a Debt Management Plan (DMP)[22] if the individual's circumstances fulfil certain criteria. Several other similar British initiatives exist in the form of telephone helplines and Web sites, for example the *Insolvency Helpline* is a national helpline also offering a comprehensive Web site for people with debt problems.[23] It is a nonprofit, independent service provided through expert advisors who give debt counselling over the telephone for individuals and businesses, and, on request, send out a "self-help information pack" free of charge.[24] There is also *Payplan (www.payplan.com)* which offers a useful Web service as well as free DMPs,[25] and *Debt Questions*, a Web site which offers a comprehensive range of advice to people with debt problems who are seeking concrete solutions.[26] An example of advisory services offered in Austria is the private, independent network of debtor advice centres, (*Schuldnerberatungsstellen*), which advises highly indebted individuals about how they can apply for private bankruptcy proceedings.These associations also tend to support, advise, and accompany consumers when the latter apply for private bankruptcy proceedings.

Web sites

Web sites and other online services are also a frequently used delivery method. In the United States, the armed forces operate one specifically targeted online group for debt advice. The United States Department of Defence's Web portal, the *LIFE Lines Services Network* was established in cooperation with the United States Navy and the Federal Trade Commission (a government agency).[27] It is a Web portal supplying a range of information to military personnel and their families, including preventive and curative advice. The LIFELines Personal Finance Section gives practical information on personal finance matters including credit management, credit cards, loans, and the resolution of credit problems. The portal provides two debt-related articles – one preventive, the other curative. Clean Up Your Credit teaches military personnel about such financial matters and concerns as obtaining copies of credit reports, how credit ratings and risk scores work, as well as explaining possessory and statutory liens, how best to make belated payments, and how to avoid bankruptcy and scams. Consolidating Debt: Painful Pitfalls Can Lurk in the Fine Print, for Navy personnel and their families, includes links to resources offering assistance with debt consolidation and general financial management. It also gives information about the various options for debt recovery and when each one might be most appropriate for the borrower's specific circumstances.

Two of the Web sites identified (both based in the United States) are provided by private sector financial services companies and offer general information on personal finance, with one focusing on credit and the other covering credit along with other topics, such as retirement financing. *Credit Talk* is an interactive Web site providing credit education for all consumers, with a particular section targeted at students and offering practical advice tailored to them.[28] The site features an online credit calculator for the borrower, which determines the length of time it could take, based on his monthly payment, for him to repay a credit card balance, and the amount he needs to allocate if he wants to pay back the balance over a shorter time period. It also offers preventive advice on budget management and credit reports, for example, and curative advice for those consumers dealing with a debt crisis. A broader, more comprehensive initiative is the online *Center for Financial Learning*.[29] The Web site aims to serve as an online learning community to help people make informed personal financial decisions through the acquisition of objective financial information. It contains a few sections particularly focusing on consumer and mortgage credit and helping consumers learn about planning for life-events, such as preparing for starting college, or buying property. The "Owning a Home" section, gives information about what the homebuyer should know before purchasing a home as well as information on the basics of home ownership. It offers advice on the steps to take prior to and during the home purchasing procedure (along with details on the amount to put down for a new home), and details on home refinancing costs. It also features a "mortgage calculator" tool. This tool enables the consumer to enter given data and then makes personalised calculations such as how much home refinancing and mortgage insurance fees will cost as well as the relative costs of fixed- or adjustable-rate mortgages, 15- or 30-year mortgage terms for the homebuyer. For each set of results calculated, the online tool advises the homebuyer of the option that will suit him best.

In Canada, an interactive Web-based mortgage calculator, called the Mortgage Qualifier Calculator, was designed by the Financial Consumer Agency of Canada (FCAC) during the years 2003-04 (FCAC, 2003-04a). Consumers can use the new mortgage qualifier calculator for several tasks such as, for example, determining whether they might qualify for the home they wish to purchase given their current debt and income levels. The calculator also shows the methods used by lenders to compute the ratios which help them choose whether a consumer can qualify for a mortgage or not. Finally the interactive tool supplies helpful tips for consumers on the appropriate actions they should take if the calculator indicates that they cannot qualify for a mortgage.

Public educational campaigns and events

Just a few examples of events, symposia, lectures, presentations and educational campaigns have been identified. Korea's regulatory and supervisory authority, the Financial Supervisory Service (FSS), offers preventive and curative advice on consumer credit in the form of lecture and presentation sessions for the residents of small- or medium-sized (often remote) towns with little access to adequate financial information. Members of FSS local branches visit the towns along with lawyers to provide financial information on FSS aims, tips for personal credit management, advice on dispute settlement cases, and information on financial transactions. They also offer guidance sessions (of around 2 hours each) on civil consumer affairs to the local residents.[30] Moreover, in 2003, the authority began a vast educational campaign on credit in the form of financial booklets and educational videotapes. A total of 45 thousand booklets[31] and a range of videotapes[32] were distributed to consumer organisations, city and county offices, financial associations, and financial companies around the country. In Austria, meanwhile, the Federal Chamber of Labour (BAK) held a symposium in September 2003 on excess indebtedness. At this event, experts from the Austrian National Bank, the Debt Advice Service offices, market researchers and psychologists were invited to report on new trends in consumer debt. Among the discussions were debt use among young people, which is on the rise owing to increased mobile phone costs, overdrawn current accounts, a greater number going into higher education, and a lack of awareness about money management.

Training courses and seminars

Very few initiatives offering training programmes and counselling sessions have been identified. In the United States, the *Money Smart curriculum*, a financial education training curriculum and course offered at national level, adopts a broadly preventive approach to provide consumer and mortgage debt education (ECI Africa Consulting, 2004; Burhouse *et al.*, 2004; Autumn *et al.*, 2003). Provided by a partnership between two government departments/ agencies (United States Department of Labour and the Federal Deposit Insurance Corporation – FDIC), it delivers information that aims to build fundamental financial literacy skills for mainly disadvantaged consumers with credit problems. Through providing information to familiarise households with basic financial fundamentals, including credit, loans, savings, and home ownership, it aims to improve financial literacy, help enhance consumers' money management skills, and build their financial confidence to use credit services effectively. The curriculum is comprised of ten instructor-led and comprehensive training modules (of 1 hour each) covering fundamental financial topics, five of which are related to consumer and mortgage credit:

- introduction to credit;
- how your credit history affects your credit future;

- how to make a credit card work for you;
- know what you are borrowing before you buy; and
- home ownership.

The programme is commended by experts, first, for the flexibility of its delivery (it can be taught in its entirety or specific modules can fill in gaps in other financial education programmes); second, for the fact that it is offered free of charge to financial education providers interested in delivering credit education in their communities; and third, because it is available in several languages other than English (Spanish, Korean, Chinese, Vietnamese). The results of the course as of 2003 were positive: by June 2003, 50 000 consumers had become familiar with the curriculum. By November 2003, the FDIC had forged partnerships with 626 organisations to provide the course, and had distributed 99 000 curricula copies. For 2006, an ambitious new target has been set – for the programme to reach 1 million people. Also in the United States, a non-profit community/educational organisation, Penn State Cooperative Extension, offers a curative consumer loan education training programme called 10 Ways to Reduce Debt.[33] This programme provides Pennsylvania-based individuals, families, communities and businesses with information on a range of subjects in order to help them manage their credit more effectively and offers a thorough overview of the American credit system.

Evaluations of credit education programmes

Evaluations are extremely important for identifying those programmes that are most effective. According to the United States Consumer Bankers Association's (CBA) 2004 Survey of Bank-Sponsored Financial Literacy Programs, two-thirds of banks/partners offering or sponsoring credit counselling programmes and four-fifths of banks/partners offering or sponsoring mortgage/homeownership counselling programmes have used evaluation metrics to assess the efficacy of their programmes (CBA, 2004). Governments may wish to undertake a similar evaluation exercise.

The OECD has decided to focus on four evaluations of credit education programmes for which suitable data were available. These programmes were mostly counselling initiatives and all were conducted in the United States, which suggests a need for other countries to conduct studies, preferably on programmes using other methods besides counselling. All four initiatives considered involved objective or subjective follow-up study. The evaluations offer some indications for what works and what does not in credit education. Although they highlight the best and most cost-effective delivery methods for financial training on mortgage or consumer debt management, the variety of methods studied are limited (mainly counselling).

Using objective follow-up measures

- **Evaluation of counselling component in mortgage-related programmes – Affordable Gold and Mortgage Foreclosure Prevention Program (MFPP)**

In the United States, Freddie Mac, a government sponsored enterprise (GSE) carried out a study of around 40 000 mortgages taken out by borrowers under its affordable housing loan programme, *Affordable Gold*, from 1993 through 1998 (Hirad and Zorn, 2002). Pre-purchase counselling from a variety of sources, including mortgage insurers, government bodies, and nonprofit groups, had been given to some borrowers in the programme but not to others, with clients' mortgage payment performance representing a measure of the success of this counselling. The study aimed to determine whether 90-day delinquency rates were affected by pre-purchase home ownership counselling or not, and whether effectiveness of the counselling varied with any course format variations (individual counselling, telephone counselling, group classes or home study). The 90-day delinquency rate was 19 per cent lower, on average, among borrowers who had received counselling than among similar borrowers who had not. The delinquency rate among those who had received individual counselling was 34 per cent lower than among those who had not. Among those who had received classroom and home study training, delinquency rates were down 26 and 21 per cent respectively, with telephone counselling failing to bring down delinquency rates at all. This study concludes that financial counselling can be effective in reducing mortgage delinquency.

The *Mortgage Foreclosure Prevention Program* (MFPP) in the United States, was a training/counselling programme focusing on mortgage credit and offering post-purchase advice (Mallach, no date). From 1991 to 1995, six housing finance agencies supplied services to more than 1 500 households in four American states. As well as curative counselling, the MFPP provided preventive financial support for households to meet mortgage payment requirements. Objective studies carried out by the Wilder Research Center, an independent nonprofit centre, looked at two groups of households, both of which received counselling and one of which also received financial assistance. Participants in the group that received financial assistance along with counselling were more likely to avoid foreclosure than those in the group that did not (Mallach, no date). Unfortunately there was no control group consisting of individuals who did not receive any counselling. Thus, it was impossible to assess the impact of counselling on the avoidance of foreclosure.

- **Credit Counselling Activities**

In the United States, a study of National Foundation for Credit Counseling (NFCC) activities in 1997 was conducted by the Credit Research Center,

Georgetown University (Elliehausen *et al.*, 2002). The study notes that, in 2000, over 880 000 new clients were counselled by NFCC member agencies – over twice the number counselled ten years before. It also finds that, for approximately one-third of all NFCC-agency clients, the agency's intervention with creditors involves, among other forms of assistance, the arrangement of a DMP, but that, for the remaining two-thirds of counselled clients, such intervention does not involve a DMP. The importance of this study is that it looks at non-DMP counselling and its effectiveness. The report studies the impact of one-on-one counselling sessions given by five NFCC member agencies, and carried out during a five-month period in 1997, on approximately 14 000 non-DMP clients.

Results of this study indicate that financial counselling has a significant and positive impact (Elliehausen *et al.*, 2002). The effect was found to be greatest for clients who were the riskiest borrowers. In comparison to the reference group, improvement among counselled clients was generally experienced across a range of credit characteristics. Delinquency rates for counselled clients relative to the reference group, were also considerably better three years on from the counselling in 1997.[34] Moreover the risk scores of the vast majority of counselled borrowers were found to have improved during the three-year observation period, compared to other borrowers showing similar initial risk scores. Most counselled borrowers had considerably fewer credit accounts, reduced debt, and less credit delinquencies relative to other borrowers.

Using objective and subjective follow-up measures

- ### Consumer and mortgage credit education programme, MONEY 2000: objective and subjective studies

Money 2000 was a personal financial training programme conducted in more than 30 American states, and developed by the Rutgers Co-operative Extension Service, a community and educational organisation (O'Neill, 2000) (O'Neill *et al.*, 2000). The programme was designed to tackle the growing problem of over-indebtedness among American households and to foster better financial well-being among them by encouraging them to lower their household debt or to increase their savings. More specifically, the programme aimed to encourage participants to reduce debt by a fixed dollar amount. Organisers called on participants to establish financial targets (*i.e.*, a set amount of reduced debt or higher savings) ranging from one or two hundred dollars to several hundred thousands of dollars. Next Extension personnel provided programme clients with educational materials (including newsletters, Web sites, training courses, government conferences, analytical computer tools and home study sessions) and carried out biannual surveys to monitor any changes occurring in the clients' debt and asset levels. They were less interested in the specific amount of assets, income, or debt of the participants than in the amount of debt reduction and/or changes in savings achieved. Included in the definition of "debt reduction" was prepayment of the mortgage principal and payment of unsecured debts (credit cards for example). Savings changes included all new dollars saved, as well as deposits in automated mutual funds and contributions to 401(k) plans. The programme was believed to be "the only savings education programme ever launched in the United States to include such a behavioural monitoring component over an extended period of time" (O'Neill et al., 2000).

A study of *Money 2000* participants conducted during Fall 1998 surveyed a convenience sample of 520 New York and New Jersey participants, which represented a 22.7 per cent response rate of the 2 292 programme participants who had received a questionnaire. This study finds that 76.2 per cent of respondents reported that they had reduced their debt (with mean and median amounts of debt reduction of $5 680 and $2 000 respectively), while 74.3 per cent indicated that they had increased their savings (with mean and median amounts of reported increased savings of $4 824 and $1 500 respectively). Where subjective findings are concerned, 80 per cent reported their financial situation as "much better" or "somewhat better" than it was prior to joining *Money 2000*, suggesting that they felt their financial situation had changed for the better as a result of participation. Participants found the quarterly newsletter (22.5 per cent of participants), followed by "tips/advice/hints" (15.4 per cent) to be the most helpful features of the programme. As to what financial resources were helping them progress towards achieving their financial goals the most frequent ones mentioned were personal qualities, such as discipline, and action (36.5 per cent of participants). The most preferred delivery methods were, in order of preference, newsletters (two-thirds of respondents), followed by classes or seminars (46.7 per cent), fact sheets (40.6 per cent), and one-to-one counselling (29.2 per cent).[35] Of five common financial challenges, "debt/credit use/spending habits" was the most frequently mentioned by the greatest share (18.8 per cent) of respondents, who said it was their greatest financial challenge.[36] Finally, younger participants were more likely than those aged 55 and older to want information and education on credit and debt management, including those older households with dependent children.

O'Neill et al. draw the following implications for educators from the study's main findings: helping consumers manage debt is important (the main reason for enrolment in Money 2000 by participants was concern about debt reduction); supplementary self-assessment activities are useful (evidence suggests that worksheets, checklists and other self-assessment tools should be continually developed and used for participants to make a regular check of their financial situations); objective-setting is commendable, with participants making several positive comments about the structure, motivation, and accountability that it provided them (O'Neill et al., 2000). Useful and visually attractive written materials (such as newsletters and other publications) are also popular and are preferred by participants over Web sites. Further implications are that information given in class should be made available via other delivery channels such as newsletters and Web sites (although respondents attending classes found them helpful, those who found them inconveniently scheduled or located did not); and that personal contact should be encouraged (nearly 5 per cent of respondents found the amount of personal contact they had disappointing, implying that personalised outreach methods, periodic support group meetings, one-on-one financial counselling, and online financial advice are needed).

Summary of the above

The issue of credit and debt education has been a subject of growing concern among policymakers, civil society and private sector representatives during the past decade in response to rising over-indebtedness among households. Credit and debt problems, including rising household debt and excess household indebtedness, the misuse of credit cards, and predatory lending, have resulted in an increase in delinquencies and personal bankruptcies. Household debt has risen, both in absolute terms (and relative to household income), on account of several factors including low interest rates, which have facilitated rising mortgage borrowing, and the expansion of credit card use over the past decade. Households with excessive debt burdens suffer significant financial stress, and financial institutions experience major losses due to rising delinquencies and personal bankruptcies. Moreover, over-indebtedness limits the levels of consumption expenditure possible in the economy.

Among the main reasons given for over-indebtedness, surveys point to mismanagement of personal finances resulting from financial illiteracy and a lack of practical money management skills (Jentzsch, 2003). Compounding these educational insufficiencies is an additional factor: the growing complexity of the credit market makes it increasingly difficult for today's adult financial consumers to understand credit products and services and means that they too often take on an excessive number of credit arrangements, which renders them vulnerable when their income declines. Meanwhile, among young adults, the misuse of credit cards (in part due to the expansion of their use among this age group) also poses serious problems (Mattson, L. *et al.*, 2004).

With the aim of tackling this rising over-indebtedness (and related issues), various stakeholders have focused efforts on developing credit education programmes in recent years. The extent of such development has varied across countries, with a considerable number of initiatives having been established in the United Kingdom and the United States over the past decade, but fewer in Austria and Korea. Above all there remain several obstacles to the provision of credit and debt education in these countries, including: 1) a lack of public concern about such education; 2) budgetary constraints; and 3) a difficulty in evaluating programmes.[37] One solution to this problem would be to raise awareness (in the media and elsewhere) that credit education can play an essential role in preventing debt problems. If such awareness-raising efforts were made, they might encourage more money to be channelled into the programmes, and thus to a certain extent overcome existing budgetary constraints. The majority of evaluations of credit education programmes identified so far have only been conducted in the United States. Further evaluations of credit education programs in other OECD countries are therefore needed.

Figure C.1. **Household debt to income ratio**

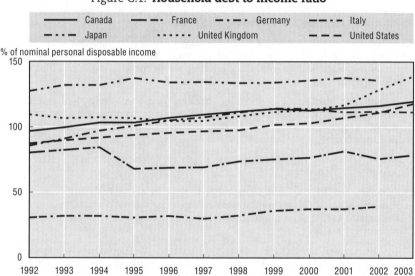

Note: Households include non-profit institutions serving households. Household liabilities are amounts outstanding at the end of the period, in per cent of nominal disposable income.

Source: OECD (2004), *OECD Economic Outlook*, No. 76, December, Annex Table 58, OECD, Paris.

Notes

1. Federal Reserve Statistical Release: *www.federalreserve.gov/releases/g19/current/default.htm*.

2. The household Debt Service Ratio (DSR) is an estimate of debt payments to disposable personal income, and the Financial Obligations Ratio (FOR) adds to the household Debt Service Ratio automobile lease payments, rental payments on tenant-occupied property, homeowners' insurance, and property tax payments (*www.federalreserve.gov/releases/housedebt/default.htm*).

3. *www.oenb.at/isaweb/report.do?&lang=EN&report=8.3.2*.

4. Responses of the CMF delegates to the OECD's 2004 questionnaire on financial education.

5. *www.oenb.at/isaweb/report.do?&lang=EN&report=8.3.2.*

6. Based on data from Thompson Financial Datastream.

7. Moreover, even though mortgage lenders set a ceiling on mortgage lending as a proportion of disposable income, they tend to raise these ceilings as mortgage rates decline.

8. Rising house prices raise the collateral values of houses allowing property owners to borrow greater amounts against these higher values of their homes (Debelle, 2004; Reserve Bank of Australia, 2003; Davey, 2001).

9. Following a study into the £4.8 bn sector in the United Kingdom, the Office of Fair Trading (OFT) referred the supply of storecard services to the Competition Commission. This comes after retailers were criticised over the way they run their storecards. The OFT concluded that features of the storecard market "prevent, restrict or distort competition" (BBC News story, "Probe into Store Card Options", *http://news.bbc.co.uk/1/hi/business/3522134.stm*).

10. Lenders accepting low client credit scores (*i.e.* lending to high-risk borrowers) so fixing higher interest rates than for products offered to those who have good credit histories. Unlike predatory lending, subprime lending is not illegal. (For more information, see Chapter 6 and Annex C.)

11. Individual insolvencies include bankruptcy and Individual Voluntary Arrangements (IVAs). IVAs are formal agreements between debtors and creditors. An IVA proposal sets out how debtors will repay their creditor s (usually over a period of five years).

12. Responses to the first OECD questionnaire on financial education, sent out in July 2003.

13. A survey by the National Consumers League in 2002 which suggested that a majority of teens (58 per cent of total survey respondents) planned to obtain their first credit card before graduating from college (*www.nclnet.org/moneyandcredit/teensurvey1.htm*).

14. In the United States, for example, regulatory developments – namely the Community Reinvestment Act – have provided incentives for financial institutions to participate in financial education programmes voluntarily (*Office* of the Comptroller of the Currency Web site).

15. Unless otherwise indicated, the information in this section comes from the responses of the CMF delegates to the OECD's questionnaire on financial education.

16. However, the OECD recognises that other OECD countries besides the aforementioned also provide credit and debt education programs, such as Canada and Spain. The reader should refer to the Appendices for further details.

17. They include national nonprofits, community-based organisations and consumer protection groups.

18. *www.cml.org.uk.*

19. Also selected brochures published by the Financial Consumer Agency of Canada (References: FCAC, 2003-04b).

20. *www.nationaldebtline.co.uk.*

21. In the United Kingdom, there are voluntary sector initiatives, many supported by lenders, designed to help consumers manage credit sensibly and address acute crises. The Money Advice Trust is an example of one of these voluntary sector organisations, and is concerned mainly with debt support. The key components of its work are National Debtline; making sure that good quality money advice is given; fundraising activities; and the promotion of change (*www.moneyadvicetrust.org*).

22. A DMP allows the debtor "to make reduced repayments to his lenders (creditors) over a number of years. Payments are made until the debt is cleared in full or until he is able to make the full repayments again. The repayments are based on what he can afford after a realistic income and expenditure has been drawn up" (*www.insolvencyhelpline.co.uk*).

23. *www.insolvencyhelpline.co.uk*.

24. *www.youthinformation.com*.

25. *www.youthinformation.com*.

26. One of the United Kingdom's largest debt management companies, Payplan works in conjunction with nonprofits (*e.g.* Paylink Trust, National Debtline etc.) to help borrowers who have unmanageable debts. It uses a specially developed system to make repayment arrangements between creditors and their debtors. Its Web site, meanwhile, provides practical advice and tips for individuals to resolve their debt problems (*www.payplan.com*).

27. *www.lifelines.navy.mil* (Personal Finances section).

28. *www.creditalk.com*.

29. *www.financiallearning.com*.

30. With respect to follow-up/evaluation, generally no participant follow-up survey/ evaluation process has been required by the Korean FSS following these lectures.

31. With suggestions for financial transactions, tips for personal credit management, information on the legal aid system and cases of dispute settlement.

32. Including suggestions for credit card use, the prevention of damage from private financing, and so on. For more information, details of this videotape are available on the Korean FSS' English language Web site: *http://english.fss.or.kr/en/englishIndex.jsp*.

33. *www.nefe.org/amexeconfund/materials/tenwaystoreducedebt.html*.

34. Delinquency experience was measured by the reduction in 30+ and 60+ day delinquencies over the last 12 months of this three-year observation period.

35. These percentages exceed 100 per cent because multiple responses were provided.

36. Including low income/loss of income/irregular income, unexpected expenses/high expenses/emergencies, children/children's expenses/family, and personal qualities.

37. Responses of the CMF delegates to the OECD's 2004 questionnaire on financial education.

References

Austrian National Bank (ANB) (2003a), *Financial Stability Report 5*, Austrian National Bank (Oesterreichische Nationalbank – OeNB), Vienna, Austria, *www.oenb.at/en/ img/fsr_05_tcm16-8063.pdf*, accessed February 2005.

Austrian National Bank (ANB) (2003b), "The real economy and financial markets in Austria", *Financial Stability Report 6*, Austrian National Bank (Oesterreichische Nationalbank – OeNB), Vienna, Austria, *www.oenb.at/en/img/fsr6_realeconomy_tcm16-9499.pdf*, accessed February 2005.

Autumn, S. *et al.* (2003), "Bringing the Unbanked into the Financial Services Market", Consumer Interests Annual, Vol. 40, *http://consumerinterests.org/public/articles/Unbanked_03.pdf*, accessed 16th January 2004.

Braunstein, S. and C. Welch (2002), "Financial Literacy: An Overview of Practice, Research and Policy", *Federal Reserve Bulletin*, Washington D.C., *www.federalreserve.gov/pubs/bulletin/2002/1102lead.pdf#*, accessed 22 August 2003.

Burhouse, S., D. Gambrell and A. Harris (2004), "Delivery Systems for Financial Education in Theory and Practice", *FYI: An Update on Emerging Issues in Banking*, Federal Deposit Insurance Corporation (FDIC), United States, 22 September, *www.fdic.gov/bank/analytical/fyi/2004/092204fyi.html*, accessed February 2005.

Christenbury, J.H. and N.M. Porter (1999), "Money 2000: A Model Extension Program", *Journal of Extension*, Vol. 37, No. 1, February 1999, *www.joe.org/joe/1999february/a1.html*, accessed March 2005.

Citizens' Advice Bureau (CAB) (2001), *Summing Up: Bridging the Financial Literacy Divide*, *www.citizensadvice.org.uk/financialdivide.pdf*, accessed December 2004.

Consumer Bankers Association (CBA) (2004), 2004 Survey of Bank-Sponsored Financial Literacy Programs, *www.cbanet.org/SURVEYS/literacy/documents/WEB%20FINAL%202004%20Financial%20Literacy%20Survey%20Report.pdf*, accessed March 2005.

Consumer Federation of America (CFA) (2000), "Facts about Consumer Credit Card Debt and Bankruptcy", *http://nacba.org/108_congress/pdfs/Credit_Card_Debt_Bankruptcy.pdf*, accessed January 2005.

Davey, M. (2001), "Mortgage equity withdrawal and consumption", *Quarterly Bulletin*, Spring 2001, Bank of England, Bank of England Publications, London, United Kingdom, *www.bankofengland.co.uk/publications/quarterlybulletin/qb010105.pdf*, accessed February 2005.

Debelle, G. (2004a), "Macroeconomic implications of rising household debt", *Working Paper*, No. 153, Bank for International Settlements (BIS), Basel, Switzerland, *www.oenb.at/isaweb/report.do?&lang=EN&report=8.3.2*, accessed February 2005.

Debelle, G. (2004b), "Household Debt and the Macroeconomy", *BIS Quarterly Review*, March 2004, Bank for International Settlements (BIS), Basel, Switzerland, *www.bis.org/publ/qtrpdf/r_qt0403e.pdf*, accessed March 2005.

Durkin, T.A. (2000), "Credit Cards: Use and Consumer Attitudes, 1970-2000", *Federal Reserve Bulletin*, September 2000, Board of Governors of the Federal Reserve System, Washington D.C., *www.federalreserve.gov/pubs/bulletin/2000/0900lead.pdf*, accessed Febuary 2005.

ECI Africa Consulting (ECI) (2004), *FinMark Trust: Financial Literacy Scoping Study and Strategy Report*, *www.finmarktrust.org.za/documents/2004/AUGUST/FinLit_Report.pdf*, accessed December 2004.

Elliehausen, G.E., C. Lundquist and M.E. Staten (2002), "The Impact of Credit Counseling on Subsequent Borrower Credit Usage and Payment Behavior", Credit Research Center, *Monograph #36*, Georgetown University, *http://inchargefoundation.com/_assets/research_reports_and_publications/42.pdf*, accessed 27 June 2003.

European Commission (EC) (2002), "Consumer credit rules for the 21st century", Press Release, 11 September 2002, *http://europa.eu.int/rapid/pressReleasesAction.do?reference=IP/02/ 1289&format=HTML&aged=0&language=EN&guiLanguage=en*, accessed January 2005.

Financial Consumer Agency of Canada (FCAC) (2003-04a), *Value for Canadians*, Annual Report, *www.fcac-acfc.gc.ca/AnnualReports/2003_2004/eng/contents.asp*, accessed July 2005.

Financial Consumer Agency of Canada (FCAC) (2003-04b), selected brochures in the *Credit Cards and You kit, including: Getting the Most from Your Credit Card; Playing it Safe: How to Protect Your Credit Card and Credit History; Your Rights and Responsibilities: The Cost of Borrowing with a Credit Card and Managing Your Money; How to Save with a Credit Card, www.fcac-acfc.gc.ca/eng/publications/ccc/0104/default.asp*, accessed July 2005.

Hawke, J.D. Jr. (2002), "Financial Literacy: A Key to New Banking Markets", Speech prepared by the Comptroller of the Currency before the Consumer Bankers Association, Arlington, Virginia, April 8, *www.cbanet.org/Issues/Financial_Literacy/ documents/HawkeFinLitSpeech.pdf*, accessed December 2004.

Hirad, A. and P.M. Zorn (2001), "A Little Knowledge is a Good Thing: Empirical Evidence of the Effectiveness of Pre-Purchase Homeownership Counselling", paper presented at the conference on Sustainable Community Development; What Works, What Doesn't and Why, sponsored by the Federal Reserve System, Washington D.C., 27-28 March 2003, *www.chicagofed.org/cedric/files/ 2003_conf_paper_session1_zorn.pdf*, accessed February 2005.

Hopley, V. (2003), "Financial Education: What is it and What Makes it So Important?", *Community Reinvestment Report*, series, No. 1, Federal Reserve Bank of Cleveland, *www.clevelandfed.org/CommAffairs/CR_Reports/CRreport.pdf*, accessed 30 July 2003.

Jentzsch, N. (2003), "The Implications of the New Consumer Credit Directive for EU Credit Market Integration", *Position Paper*, Freie Universität Berlin, Berlin, *www.europarl.eu.int/hearings/20030429/juri/jentzsch1_en.pdf*, accessed February 2005.

Mallach, A. (no date), "Homeownership Education and Counseling: Issues in Research and Definition", *Community Affairs*, for the Federal Reserve Bank of Philadelphia, *www.phil.frb.org/cca/capubs/homeowner.pdf*, accessed February 2005.

Marcuss, M., (2004), "A Look at Household Bankruptcies", *Communities and Banking*, Spring 2004 issue, Federal Reserve Bank of Boston, *www.bos.frb.org/commdev/c&b/ 2004/Spring/Bankruptcies.pdf*, accessed March 2005.

Mattson, L. *et al.* (2004), "Variables Influencing Credit Card Balances of Students at Mid-western University", *NASFAA Journal of Student Financial Aid*, *www.nasfaa.org/ annualpubs/journal/Vol34n2/mattson.pdf*, accessed February 2005.

Mavrinac, S. and C.W. Ping (2004), "Financial Education for Women in Asia Pacific", paper presented at the CITIGROUP/INSEAD Women's Financial Education Summit, 2 November 2004, Hong Kong, China, *www.insead.edu/discover_INSEAD/documents/ WFEWorkingPaper.pdf*, accessed March 2005.

National Endowment for Financial Education (NEFE) (2002), "Financial Literacy In America: Individual Choices, National Consequences", *White Paper* summarising issues discussed at the National Endowment for Financial Education (NEFE) symposium: The State of Financial Literacy in America – Evolutions and Revolutions, Denver, Colorado, 9-11 October 2002, *www.nefe.org/pages/ whitepaper2002symposium.html*, accessed Febuary 2005.

151

National Statistics United Kingdom (NSUK) (2005), "UK population grows to 59.6 million", 28 January, *www.statistics.gov.uk/cci/nugget.asp?id=760*, accessed March 2005.

New Economics Foundation United Kingdom (NEF) (2004), "New Banking Partnership Sounds Death Knell For Predatory Lenders", *Online News Article*, 16 December, *www.neweconomics.org/gen/news_communitybankingpartnership.aspx*, accessed February 2005.

OECD (2000), *OECD Economic Outlook*, No. 68, December, OECD, Paris.

OECD (2004a), *Economic Survey of Korea*, Volume 2004/10, OECD, Paris.

OECD (2004b), *OECD Economic Outlook*, No. 76, December, OECD, Paris.

O'Neill, B. (2000), *How Clients Handle Money: Research Results and Implications*, Rutgers Cooperative Extension, State University of New Jersey at Rutgers, *www.rce.rutgers.edu/money/pdfs/handlemoney.pdf*, accessed 28 June 2004.

O'Neill, B. *et al.* (2000), "Money 2000: Feedback From and Impact on Participants", *Journal of Extension*, Vol. 38, No. 6, *www.joe.org/joe/2000december/rb3.html*, accessed 28 June 2004.

Reserve Bank of Australia (RBA) (2003), "Household Debt: What the Data Show", Reserve Bank of Australia *Bulletin*, March 2003, *www.rba.gov.au/PublicationsAndResearch/Bulletin/bu_mar03/bu_0303_1.pdf*, accessed February 2005.

Stegman, M.A. (2003), "Banking the Unbanked: Connecting Residents of Social Housing to the Financial Mainstream", in R. Forrest and J. Lee (eds.), *Housing and Social Change: East-West Perspectives*, Routledge, London, *www.kenan-flagler.unc.edu/assets/documents/CC_Routledge-2003%20BankingUnbanked.pdf*, accessed December 2004.

UK Department of Trade and Industry (UKDTI) and Department for Work and Pensions (UKDWP) (2004), *Tackling Over-Indebtedness Action Plan 2004*, United Kingdom, *www.dti.gov.uk/ccp/topics1/pdf1/overdebt0704.pdf*, accessed February 2005.

UK Department of Trade and Industry (UKDTI) (2005), "2. Individual Insolvencies in England and Wales", *Statistics Release*, Statistics and Analysis Directorate, United Kingdom, 6 May, *www.dtistats.net/sd/insolv/table2.htm*, accessed 20 May 2005.

Weston, L.P. (no date), "The Truth About Credit Card Debt", *MSN Money Online*, *http://moneycentral.msn.com/content/Banking/creditcardsmarts/P74808.asp*, accessed February 2005.

Willis, M. (2004), Opening Address Given by the Executive Vice President of J.P. Morgan Chase and Co. at the Federal Reserve Bank of Dallas' Conference, The Business of Immigrant Markets: Providing Financial Access to Services, Dallas, Texas, 29 September 2004,
www.jpmorganchase.com/cm/BlobServer?blobtable=Document&blobcol=urlblob&blobkey=name&blobheader=application/pdf&blobwhere=jpmc/community/grants/willis092904.pdf, accessed April 2005.

Yon-Se, K. (2004), "Elderly credit defaulters hit seven-month high", *The Korea Times*, 23 December.

Internet References

Austrian National Bank (ANB): [*www.oenb.at*] (accessed January 2005).

BBC News Web site: [*http://news.bbc.co.uk/*] (accessed March 2005).

Center for Financial Learning: [*www.financiallearning.com*] (accessed February 2005).

Council of Mortgage Lenders, UK: [*www.cml.org.uk*] (accessed January 2005).

Credit Talk: [*www.creditalk.com*] (accessed February 2005).

Department of Trade and Industry, United Kingdom, Economics and Statistics Web site: [*www.dtistats.net*] (accessed February 2005).

Federal Reserve Board Statistics Page: Releases and Historical Data: [*www.federalreserve.gov/releases*] (accessed February 2005).

Insolvency Helpline, UK: [*www.insolvencyhelpline.co.uk*] (accessed January 2005).

Korean FSS' Web site: [*http://english.fss.or.kr/en/englishIndex.jsp*] (accessed February 2005).

Lifelines Services Network: [*www.lifelines.navy.mil*] (accessed February 2005).

Money Advice Trust: [*www.moneyadvicetrust.org*] (accessed January 2005).

National Consumers League (results of a survey conducted in 2002: "2002 Teens and Financial Education": [*www.nclnet.org/moneyandcredit/teensurvey1.htm* – in 2002] (accessed March 2005).

National Debtline, UK: [*www.nationaldebtline.co.uk*] (accessed January 2005).

National Endowment for Financial Education, United States (Information on Ten Ways to Reduce Debt programme): *www.nefe.org/amexeconfund/materials/ tenwaystoreducedebt.html*.

National Statistics, United Kingdom: [*www.statistics.gov.uk*] (accessed March 2005).

National Youth Agency, UK: [*www.youthinformation.com*] (accessed February 2005).

Office of the Comptroller of the Currency Web site (Community Reinvestment Act Information page): [*www.occ.treas.gov/crainfo.htm*] (accessed February 2005).

Office of Financial Education: [*www.treas.gov/offices/domestic-finance/financial-institution/fin-education/overview.shtml*] (accessed February 2005).

Payplan: [www.*payplan*.com] (accessed February 2005).

ANNEX D

The Unbanked: Additional Information

Background

Defining the unbanked population

Among the four countries examined, the United States has the largest proportion of the population without a checking or savings account, estimated at 10 per cent of the population, or over 28 million individuals (USFRB Chicago, 2001). The United Kingdom follows with 8 per cent of the population who are unbanked (8 per cent of individuals and 8 per cent of households) or about 2½ to 3½ million adults that have neither a current nor a savings account (Kempson *et al.*, 2004). By contrast, only 3 per cent of adults lack an "everyday" banking account in Australia according to a survey of adult financial literacy conducted in the years 2002-03 by the ANZ Banking Group (ANZ Banking Group, 2003, cited Kempson *et al.*, 2004), and in Canada 3 to 4 per cent of adults aged over 18 have no bank account of any sort (ACEF-Centre, 1996 and Ekos, 1998, cited Kempson *et al.*, 2004). In Australia, the relatively low percentage is mainly due to an almost entirely automated electronic transfer system in which benefits paid by direct deposit into a bank account are the norm. Nevertheless there is increasing concern about the "underbanked" or "underserved" in Australia.

In the United States, unbanked households are from diverse population groups, including: low-income; racial and ethnic minorities (such as African-Americans, Hispanics and Asians); new immigrants, refugees and asylees; and the indigenous population (Native Americans) (Autumn *et al.*, 2003). In Australia, the groups most likely to suffer financial exclusion are the low-income in urban areas, inhabitants of remote and isolated rural areas (of which 600 communities are estimated to be without access to financial institutions), indigenous consumers, and immigrants (Connolly and Hajaj, 2001). In the United Kingdom, minorities and immigrants (African Caribbean, Pakistani and Bangladeshi) are disproportionately likely to be unbanked, particularly Pakistani and Bangladeshi women, and account-holding is found at its lowest levels in inner-city and deprived areas (Kempson and Whyley, 1998, and the UK OFT, 1999, cited Kempson *et al.*, 2004). In Canada,. a larger proportion (8 to 10 per cent) of unbanked individuals are found among low earners – earning under $25,000 CAD annually (Ekos, 1998; Morris and Phillips, 1999; Environics 2000, cited Kempson *et al.*, 2004). Research also finds that several of the unbanked are Native Canadians (Buckland *et al.*, 2003, cited Kempson *et al.*, 2004). It should also be noted that, across the four countries, aggravating factors – such as unemployment, low incomes, high levels of deprivation, disabilities, and literacy, learning and language difficulties – worsen financial exclusion and make these groups more vulnerable to other forms of exclusion (including social exclusion).

Factors heightening the importance of financial exclusion as an issue

Demographic trends are highlighted by data found in the 2000 census which show that the population of the United States has become far more varied, with foreign-born households making up a major "consumer market force" (Braunstein and Welch, 2002). The census shows a particular increase in the number of Hispanics/Latinos, with this growth set to continue for the future so that by 2009 they will represent a key market for financial services (with their purchasing power at $1.1 trillion).[1] In the United Kingdom, meanwhile, net inward foreign migration from non European Union countries has more than doubled since 1997 to 233 000 in 2002.[2] These non-native groups in both countries tend to lack access to mainstream financial systems, may be unfamiliar with native financial practices or may not speak the native language.

Governments and society now increasingly require individuals to be responsible for their own financial well-being in many aspects of everyday life. This is illustrated most markedly by the changes in welfare reform since the mid 1990s (known as the Welfare-to-Work policies in the United Kingdom), which shifted the unemployed away from the status of government benefit recipients to "permanent job seekers" and in many cases low-income earners – referred to as the "working poor" in the United States (Partee, 2001; Stegman, 1998).

Simultaneously with these welfare reforms, the transfer in the late 1990s to making all government payments electronically has meant that consumers need to have a bank account in order to be able to receive government pay and benefits. In the United Kingdom, electronic transfer has resulted in the introduction of "basic bank accounts" (Stegman, 1998; Kempson *et al.*, 2004). The United States initiated its Electronic Transfer Account (ETA) in 1999 via participating federally insured financial institutions, and in the same year the United Kingdom initiated "basic bank accounts" following the introduction of Automated Credit Transfer (ACT) payments[3] (Kempson *et al.*, 2004). Meanwhile, in Australia, by the late 1990s, all four major banks (ANZ, National

Australia Bank, Commonwealth Bank and Westpac) were already offering basic bank accounts (Kempson et al., 2004). In Canada, regulations providing for access to basic banking services were included in Bill C-8, which was enacted in June 2001 and took effect on September 30th 2003 (Kempson et al., 2004). These developments mean that, by the beginning of the 21st century, having a bank account and understanding electronic banking were no longer mere conveniences but prerequisites for engaging in the economic process in a self-responsible, autonomous fashion (Kempson et al., 2004).

Benefits of financial education for the unbanked

Although regulatory protections and legal remedies remain important, financial education programmes are considered an essential element for successfully combating and preventing sub-prime and predatory lending in disadvantaged communities (Malkin, 2003). Financial education initiatives have also been recommended as a means of helping borrowers better comprehend mortgage credit fundamentals and of contributing to the better prevention of predatory lending, for example, following a variety of efforts[4] in 1999 and 2000 by United States federal and local agencies to obtain information on abusive lending practices (Braunstein and Welch, 2002). Finally, the value of financial education programmes for fostering savings and the use of savings accounts among these communities was a point highlighted recently by United States Federal Reserve Board Chairman, Alan Greenspan, "[Financial] education and training programmes may be the most critical service offered…to enhance the ability of lower-income households to accumulate assets. Indeed analysts have shown that a comprehensive understanding of basic principles of budgeting and saving, at the start, increases household wealth in later years" (Greenspan, 2002).

Description and assessment of financial education programmes for the un/underbanked[5]

Selected programmes

Below are a selection of programmes that tackle financial exclusion, marginalisation, and low financial skills, and span all personal reasons and related issues for lack/underuse of mainstream bank accounts. Programmes are organised by type of delivery method used. This list is not exhaustive, but aims to give some descriptions of representative programmes.

Training courses

Three training courses are described: one introducing electronic banking to the elderly; the other assisting a majority indigenous audience to manage

156

income and achieve improved living standards and the other training prospective Native American homebuyers. The *Self Service Banking and Older Australians* initiative in Australia aimed to provide elderly consumers with practical experience in using electronic banking technology to help them understand and feel more familiar with it (ADoHA, 1999). The course used a face-to-face training delivery method offered through self service banking seminars (ABA, 2000b). Instructors were bank representatives who gave training to participants on a wide range of topics related to electronic banking including how to use ATMs, electronic funds transfer at point of sale (EFTPOS), telephone and Internet banking (Kempson *et al.*, 2004; ABA, 2000a). Providers included federal government, trade associations and local community groups. The programme involved the establishment of "joint community-bank working parties investigating the physical, psychological and opportunity barriers to greater use of new banking technologies by older Australians" (Australian DoHA, 1999; ABA, 2004). Also in Australia the *Cape York Family Income Management Project* is a training course providing information and assistance to underserved indigenous people on family budget planning and skills, debt management, using bank accounts, bill paying, loans and purchasing decisions. Covering the Cape York area of North Queensland it aims to help stabilise family functioning, reduce financial stress and conflict, ensure better health and living standards, and assist individuals to identify and discharge responsibilities to each other.[6] One ultimate goal is to provide information and recommendations to relevant government bodies on financial education to this population. The project is overseen by a Family Income Management (FIM) working group comprising diverse government and community groups, and is funded by the federal government. As of May 2003, the initiative had 549 active participants and of these, 429 had reached the savings goals set.[7] The programme has demonstrated numerous social and economic benefits for participants and the wider community. Helping families cover essential living costs and save for future needs contributes to increasing motivation to train and work for higher incomes. It also contributes to building consumer capacity, thus helping to ensure the viability of local enterprises. Stabilising family functioning helps to increase school attendance and achievement. With the Cape York Family Income Management project having proved a success, the Government will provide funding of a total $4.4 million over four years starting July 2004 for additional financial literacy and money management projects to be established in other Indigenous communities.[8]

In the United States, the Hawaiian training programme series (called *Kahua Waiwai*, or Foundation for Wealth) aims to promote access to capital for Hawaiian native communities and to increase their capacity to achieve economic self-sufficiency.[9] Provided by Hawaiian Community Assets (HCA), a non-profit organisation, *Kahua Waiwai* adopts a broad "holistic approach" in response to the particular cultural differences of Native communities, namely by incorporating traditional community values and resource management practices into financial education (Malkin, 2003). It focuses on those subjects of specific concern to the indigenous population (home ownership and mortgage counselling) using a sustainable approach and offering counselling before, during and after home purchase. One initiative, the *Kahua Waiwai Homelands Development Programme*, has had particularly good results. It has produced an unusually high mortgage pre-qualification rate for households, many of whom had been waiting up to 40 years to qualify or had failed to qualify for a mortgage at all.[10] These goals are achieved partly through partnership with other local nonprofits and IDA[11] savings programmes.[12]

The OECD identified three programmes in Canada combining IDAs with financial literacy and management training. The first programme, Learn$ave, developed and managed by Social and Enterprise Development Innovations (SEDI), is the largest demonstration of individual development accounts (IDAs) in the world (SEDI, 2004). It aims to test whether IDAs are an effective means through which to provide finance education and training to low-income adults. It includes ten case study project sites: of these, seven provide participants with both a financial incentive to save in the IDA and a minimum 15 hours of financial management training including budgeting, credit, banking and development of a savings plan. There are also three experimental sites in which there is a random assignment of participants to one of three groups for comparison purposes: the first group receives a traditional IDA program with both financial incentives to save and 15 hours of financial management training, the second group works only towards the IDA financial incentive and the third group is a comparison group with neither saving incentive nor training. With regards to the scope of the project, all sites together involve 4 875 participants and the programme is being evaluated by researchers at the Social Research and Demonstration Corporation. The experimental sites are expected to provide information on the relationship between training and savings outcomes in IDA programmes. However, the project is still in its early stages and as yet no firm conclusions can be drawn as to this relationship.

The second programme, Fair Gains, is an IDA and financial training programme offered by a non-profit organisation at local level in Calgary (SEDI, 2004). It targets low-income inhabitants keen to save towards such goals as business development, homeownership, and further education and skills training (both for themselves and/or their children). It receives its funding through a non-profit, a private sector grouping and one anonymous donor. As well as the basic money management areas covered, other topics delivered include, insurance, wills and estate planning, taxes and information on the world economy. The third programme, is also delivered at community level and is provided by a community organisation, SEED Winnipeg (SEDI, 2004). Its funding is supplied by a non-profit organisation, a provincial government, and other private financers. Asset purchase goals are similar to the Calgary program described above but also include saving towards housing renovations as specific goals. The programme is targeted to an audience composed of predominantly urban-dwelling Aboriginals and spans topics such as problem solving, banking and credit. For those participants who hope to save to buy a home, workshops on "asset-specific" topics and peer support groups on "rights and responsibilities under social assistance" are also provided.

Two train-the-trainer programmes have also been identified, one addressing the lack of (or poor) basic financial skills and the other helping to build assets. The British-based *Train the Trainers Programme for Financial Literacy* for example, launched in 2004 and running until March 2005, was provided by the government's Basic Skills Agency (BSA) and is part of the BSA's Financial Literacy Project.[13] Financial literacy educators were trained to deliver a professional development module to other practitioners, particularly teachers of basic numeracy skills in the context of finance. This involved three parts of a chain: BSA trainers taught teacher trainers to train numeracy skill school teachers to deliver BSA modular programmes. With the programme coming to an end in March 2005, the aim was to upskill around 100 existing teacher trainers, so that the modules could be further transmitted by them to teachers in the community, thus giving the programme an ongoing aspect despite its completion later in 2005. The programme reached around 105 trainers of literacy and numeracy teachers and funding was also channelled into residential provision, media promotion, travel and events. The American national *IDA Financial Literacy Initiative* aims to connect the expanding field of IDAs with financial literacy training. It does this by providing IDA practitioners and instructors with training sessions that offer them the appropriate knowledge, expertise and materials necessary to give IDA financial literacy classes and deliver quality financial education of a practical nature.[14] Providers include non-profits and a GSE-run foundation, and the Initiative also benefits from the know-how of financial literacy experts, academics, foundations and community organisation practitioners. It uses a variety of resources such as a printed curriculum[15] (Finding Paths to Prosperity), a Participant Workbook,[16] which is accessible to the audience's specific financial literacy levels and comprehensible to IDA participants from a range of socioeconomic backgrounds and cultures, and a trainers' guide, including a CD-ROM.[17] The CD-ROM contains all curriculum worksheets and handouts and is a particularly flexible tool enabling IDA trainers to print out only those documents needed for the particular class they are to teach. Handouts can thus be more easily tailored to each specific IDA initiative and its goals.

Multiple delivery channels

The next most frequently used form of delivery for programmes is a combination of channels. One example, the *Communities Banking for Safety* programme (begun in Dallas, Texas in 2001, and since then expanded to other cities), aims to teach immigrants about the risks of carrying cash[18] and comprises three components: i) an effort to facilitate account-opening and find alternative methods of identification;[19] ii) an outreach element, teaching about the personal risk of carrying cash, the safety and usefulness of bank accounts and ATMs, and encouraging trust among immigrants in the United States banking system;[20] iii) bilingual training in financial literacy which aims to enhance the first two efforts(Autumn *et al.*, 2003; USFRB Dallas, 2002; Williams, 2002). Delivery channels are as varied as the programme components, and include training courses for the financial education component and community meetings and presentations in Spanish for the outreach element. The programme is promoted via community seminars, festivals and health fairs, as well as through flyers, posters and brochures. Understandably, great use is also made of Hispanic media sources. The initiative has resulted in a decline in the number of theft-related crimes occurring in the targeted communities; the opening of over 1 000 bank accounts; the deposit of several $1 000; and investments in addition to standard saving accounts made by several unbanked Hispanic immigrants. The success of the programme has encouraged Police Departments in other cities (Austin, Chicago and Los Angeles, for example) to launch similar initiatives. One reason given for the programme's success is that it goes out into the community and brings the bank to the people (Autumn *et al.*, 2003).

Publications

Publications, particularly in the form of brochures available online, are also a major delivery method.[21] Here a brochure and a fact sheet are highlighted, both explaining basic banking and tackling misperceptions among the unbanked population which act as barriers to account opening. In the United States, *Helping People in Your Community Understand Basic Financial Services* is a comprehensive training brochure available online for use by community trainers with unbanked individuals.[22] It provides basic information and advice for trainers to teach about the use of bank accounts. It was published in 1998 and revised in 2000 by a government agency set up by the Department of Treasury following EFT 99 – the Financial Services Education Coalition. It contains many useful resource materials including guidelines on how to plan and deliver such a financial educational programme, sample materials (flyers and evaluation forms), a range of fact sheets for use with unbanked consumers and an outline of consumer protection laws. In Australia, a fact sheet, *How to Save on Fees and Charges*, aims to help people understand how to reduce charges when they come to use mainstream financial services, so that they are not deterred from opening accounts due to what they perceive as high charges.[23] Published and financed by the Financial Information Service of Centrelink, the government welfare agency network, the fact sheet is suitable for all consumers, but low income/disadvantaged can particularly benefit. The document explains how financial institutions make their money, and how consumers can reduce or eliminate the amounts they pay in fees and charges for three account types (checking and savings accounts, credit and debit card accounts and home and personal loans).

Advisory/counselling services

Next in the ranking of delivery channels come counselling services. One example (in the United States) is the *Greater Miami Prosperity Campaign* which informs the working poor about how best to benefit from tax credits.[24] Launched in 2002, it offers advice on the Earned Income Tax Credit (EITC) for which low-income workers are eligible. Provided by a non-profit (the Human Services Coalition), the programme is delivered in tax counselling centres and in Tax Preparation Sites at which free tax preparation is offered. Six nearby non-profits are also involved in the initiative: they promote the Prosperity Campaign, offer free tax preparation services, economic benefit screenings and other services. They also aim to connect low-wage workers to other existing economic benefits programmes available to them, such as the *Childcare Tax Credit*. The Greater Miami Prosperity Campaign is funded through a partnership between four non-profits and a federal government department.[25] The Campaign has had a certain degree of success. Within the programme's first year, EITC revenues had increased by 13% in Miami-Dade County. These funds are being spent in the local economy, generating jobs and increasing spending with an estimated multiplier of approximately 4 times. In February 2004, the programme's provider received the Department of the Treasury Certificate of Recognition for its successes in providing financial education to the community.[26]

Internet Web sites/online services

Another frequently used delivery channel is Internet Web sites/online services. Several Web sites help the generic un/underbanked understand the use and benefit of basic financial services/accounts, providing basic instruction on how to use accounts, and delivering and building basic financial literacy skills. In the United Kingdom, for example, the Financial Services Authority, FSA, offers such basic information on its Web site under the "How to" section.[27] These pages aim to deliver, build, and improve fundamental financial literacy skills, and are suitable for all unbanked population segments. The pages explain the basics, including how to calculate a budget and use a bank account. They use clear, simple language and contain interactive demonstrations to make learning extra fun for the user. The only downside might be that these pages are not easy for an individual to locate on the FSA's site. Meanwhile in the United States, a financial institution (Visa) provides and funds the Practical Money Skills for Life Web site. The site is suitable for all financially illiterate consumers, and would be particularly useful for the non English-speaking Latino segment, as it is available in Spanish. It comprises four main sections: one each for consumers, teachers, parents, and students. The consumer group offers topics on budgeting, banking, saving/investing, credit cards, debt, smart shopping, and security. There are also sections helping build financial skills related to specific life events, and additional interactive resources (games, calculators, glossaries, a banking tutor etc.). The site has received 5 awards from various general professional and professional Web designer associations as well as from the national financial literacy initiative, Jump$tart.[28]

Public educational campaigns

The OECD finds just a few financial education programmes that are offered through public educational campaigns. In Australia, the *Consumer Affairs' Indigenous Consumer Justice Campaign*, targeting indigenous consumers using the banking system for the first time, is one example. This multi-media campaign is provided by the government at state level (Northern Territory Department of Justice) and delivered through a variety of channels including educational videos, (including one about the safe use of debit cards and pin numbers), posters, flyers and advertisements on local television. A particularly commendable feature of the campaign is that it uses an individual trusted and respected by Aboriginals to deliver important financial information: a well-known and highly-esteemed Northern Territorial indigenous person (Michael Long) has been chosen as the face of the campaign and features in the video and posters.

Evaluations of financial education programmes for un/underbanked

The OECD identified only three evaluations of programmes: two in the United States and one in the United Kingdom, and all evaluating training courses. Two use objective and subjective measures but one, a train-the-trainer course in the United States, uses only a subjective approach to follow-up.

The Community Development Programme in Financial Literacy and Basic Skills

In the United Kingdom, the *Community Development Programme in Financial Literacy and Basic Skills*[29] – initiated in response to a report by the Adult Financial Literacy Advisory Group (AdFLAG) – has national scope but is implemented at community level and targets socially excluded adults with low educational levels in areas of socio-economic disadvantage. The programme draws its providers from local government, community organisations and credit unions. It is delivered through basic skills and financial literacy training courses using paper-based methods and a one-to-one approach.

An evaluation by National Foundation for Educational Research (NFER) finds overall positive results for the programme: learners expressed greater confidence about dealing with bank staff following the training, and several said they had "gained better understanding of their entitlements", were "more confident about handling money" and were "able to organise their money more effectively" (Dartnall *et al.*, 2002). They also liked the anonymity of the community centre setting and the fact that they could trust staff, and reported a progression in their basic skills, financial literacy skills and overall self-confidence.

With respect to recruitment of participants, the evaluation concludes that "recruitment is most effective when carried out face-to-face, with the help of local community groups and partner organisations", who can draw on their "existing client base". Suggested reasons for this are the good "territorial knowledge" of community-based organisations and the fact that potential learners have "an existing relationship of trust" with community organisation employees.

As regards venue or environment, the report finds that the course should be locally based because students may not be willing or able to travel long distances even with costs paid. Ideally the course "should go to where people already are", *i.e.* provide financial education courses to local groups who are a ready-constituted audience. Failing this, says the report, courses should be held in the type of venue where participants feel comfortable (*e.g.* community centres, schools, medical practitioners' surgeries, etc.).

Where delivery methods are concerned, the report highlights that paper-based methods (leaflets and posters) were not the most effective way to reach those with poor literacy skills. It recommends that methods be varied (including the use of videos along with paper-based methods, for example). Moreover, the course must be at the appropriate level and not take for granted knowledge that learners might not possess. As some potential students may not be ready to "commit to a long course", the report recommends a flexible, modular structure so that instructors and students can pick and choose elements relevant to individual needs.

Regarding marketing efforts, the report underlines that promoters must have a clear picture of the course's content and methods, and be able to "reassure those whose reluctance to participate may be based on an outdated…understanding of formal learning" (Dartnall et al., 2002).

Financial Links for Low-Income People (FLLIP)

In the United States, the FLLIP programme is also intended for an economically and educationally disadvantaged audience[30] (Anderson et al., 2002). The financial education programme is provided by community and non-profit agencies and organisations, and offers both sites that combine IDAs with financial management training (IDA sites) and sites that include financial management training only (education-only sites). The programme's aim is to encourage participants to improve their financial knowledge and behaviour, as well as, for the IDA sites, encourage them to make deposits every month so as to be eligible for the matching money offered by the IDA initiative (Anderson et al., 2004b). The programme does this through training courses operating on sites which use a specific interactive curriculum comprised of two modules – All My Money and Your Money and Your Life (Anderson et al., 2004b).

A two-year evaluation study of the FLLIP programme was conducted (Anderson et al., 2002). At the end of the first year, an initial evaluation was published and at the end of the second year a final report was published. According to the first-year evaluation published in 2002, encouraging knowledge improvements were made by all graduates (IDA and education-only), with the mean number of correct answers for graduates on the test having risen from 64.8% (pre-training) to 78.3% (post-training) (Anderson et al., 2002). In the first year, 300 participants began the course and over half (179) completed the core curriculum (Anderson et al., 2002). IDA participants tended to drop out of the course much less than non-IDA participants, implying that the incentive of matched savings encouraged people to continue with the training.

The first-year evaluation finds the course's success to lie in the following three main reasons:

Effective delivery methods were used including a curriculum which incorporated interactive exercises, handouts, user-friendliness and the presentation of complex information in a relatively clear manner)[31] and was flexible (it was left up to the discretion of each local site and community partners as to how they delivered the curriculum, allowing them to adapt it to their local audiences) (Anderson et al., 2002). The programme also involved instructors, (and on occasion guest speakers) who generally showed a "solid grasp" of the training materials offered, put the course's interactive activities to good use and were "quite successful" in engaging students (Anderson et al., 2002).

IMPROVING FINANCIAL LITERACY – ISBN 92-64-01256-7 – © OECD 2005

Creative solutions to obstacles were found. For example, a case management relationship between trainers and clients was developed, aiming to establish trust among clients and "make the training less threatening". Childcare/transportation costs were reimbursed and, in the case of one site, calculators donated. Class times were fixed as flexibly as possible, with one recruiter contacting participants prior to every class to remind them of place and start time. Students were made to feel "at ease in the training environment" by (for example) being encouraged to participate in fixing their own learning interests and needs. Certificates of completion were given to all those who completed the programme (and at some sites, receipt of the certificates enabled the participants to easily open checking and savings accounts at co-operating banks). Graduation ceremonies were sometimes organised for final sessions (Anderson *et al.*, 2002).

There was good surveying of participant knowledge both before and after the training (Anderson *et al.*, 2002). Pre-training knowledge survey results provided an indication of client training needs while post-training surveys measured knowledge gains following the FLLIP course. The levels of pre- and post-training knowledge were then compared.

The final evaluation report for the programme finds generally positive results for the courses with overall knowledge increase and behaviour change (despite some obstacles such as inconvenient class times and childcare problems) (Anderson *et al.*, 2002). It also finds that participants show a high level of satisfaction with the training: 71.8% rate the quality of the training and 80.9% the trainer performance as excellent (Anderson *et al.*, 2004a). It reports clear evidence of behaviour change following the course. Among those who were previously unbanked during training and even when training was completed, 37.8 per cent said they had opened a new checking account and 33.6 per cent had opened a "new savings account" (Anderson *et al.*, 2004a).

All My Money programme

The All My Money training curriculum (United States) is a research-based program resource from the University of Illinois Extension.[32] It is a teaching material designed to be used by financial literacy educators in order to deliver a professional development module to other financial literacy practitioners,[33] and offers instruction in financial management and consumer skills to audiences of limited financial income and means. Available in English and Spanish, the curriculum is intended to be taught by community agency and social service organisation volunteers or staff to their clients.[34]

As of 2003, over 125 staff members of Chicago's community agencies had followed the training course.[35] Before and after the training, knowledge surveys were conducted among both the community agency staff and the clients on the programme (see below).

Pre- and post-behaviour change on the All My Money Programme

• Evaluation of Clients

Following the programme, the percentage of clients reporting improvement in their money management skills was 86 per cent.[36]

Before programme (%)	After programme (%)	Behaviour
52	9	Often/almost always run out of money
32	57	Often/almost always talk about money with family
32	11	Almost always pay bills late
60	84	Often/almost always compare prices and quality before buying

Source: *www.urbanext.uiuc.edu/chicago/ar2003/fcs3.html.*

• Evaluation of Community Agency Staff

Following the programme, the percentage of agency staff reporting improvement in their money management abilities was 91 per cent (and this despite the fact that, before their training, their money management and consumer behaviours were already stronger than those of clients).[37]

Before programme (%)	After programme (%)	Behaviour
18	4	Often/almost always run out of money
38	72	Often/almost always talk about money with family
45	16	Almost always pay bills late
66	91	Often/almost always compare prices and quality before buying

Source: *www.urbanext.uiuc.edu/chicago/ar2003/fcs3.html.*

Thus it can be seen that, following the All My Money programme and among both the selected clients and agency staff, there was a considerable reduction in the number of people saying that they "often/almost always run out of money" and "almost always pay bills late". Meanwhile there was a significant rise in the number declaring that they "often/almost always talk about money with family" and "often/almost always compare prices and quality before buying". However, such surveys are limited because they are based on participants' self-assessment, and the fact that they have only studied behaviour change in a small, selected group of programme agency staff and clients and not across the entire spectrum of participants on the programme.

Notes

1. By 2050, analysts predict that Hispanics as a percentage of the US population will be double the equivalent figures for 2000 (Robles, 2004).

2. *www.migrationwatchuk.org.*

3. ACT was a decision to move benefits payments from giro to automated credit payments: it was begun in 2003 and will be completed in two years.

4. Two of these efforts were: 1) Public Hearings to obtain comments on proposed revisions to a regulation implementing the Home Ownership Equity Protection Act (*www.federalreserve.gov/events/publichearings/default.htm*) (Braunstein and Welch, 2002); and 2) a report of findings and policy recommendations concerning predatory lending released by the joint taskforce of the Department of Housing and Urban Development and of the Department of the Treasury (*www.huduser.org/publications/ hsgfin/curbing.html*) (Braunstein and Welch, 2002).

5. Unless otherwise indicated, the information in this section comes from responses to the OECD questionnaire on financial education, sent to delegates of the Committee on Financial Markets.

6. This includes increasing money spent on food, reducing spending on alcohol or gambling, and reducing vulnerability to exploitation (*www.facs.gov.au/internet/ facsinternet.nsf/indigenous/programs-fim.htm*).

7. Stocktake of Australian financial literacy programs compiled by the Treasury as part of an Inter-Departmental Committee on financial literacy.

8. *www.facs.gov.au/internet/facsinternet.nsf/aboutfacs/budget/budget2004- 09_indigenous_financial_management.htm.*

9. *www.ruralisc.org/hca_history.htm.*

10. *www.ruralisc.org/hca_strategies.htm.*

11. Individual Development Account programmes: these aim to encourage low-income consumers to save by helping them establish saving accounts and by matching their deposits.

12. *www.ruralisc.org/hca_strategies.htm.*

13. Personal communication with Paul Worrall, head of BSA's Financial Literacy Project, UK, January 2005.

14. *www.idanetwork.org/index.php?section=initiatives&page=financial_literacy_initiative.html* and *www.ctdol.state.ct.us/ida/dir/finedu.html.*

15. *www.ctdol.state.ct.us/ida/dir/finedu.html.*

16. This workbook contains practical information on money management and financial planning (*www.idanetwork.org/index.php?section=initiatives&page= financial_literacy_initiative.html*).

17. The guide includes session outlines, handouts, guides for visual aids, and information on providing effective training sessions (*www.idanetwork.org/ index.php?section=initiatives&page=financial_literacy_initiative.html*).

18. Immigrants are very likely to lack the two forms of identification generally required to open a bank account.

19. This component involves selected banks which have facilitated account-opening for Mexican immigrants. Applicants with no or minimal credit history may qualify, and the banks will require two specific forms of identification to open checking/savings accounts, but not the (usually) necessary social security number.

20. This component involves Dallas City Police Department, the Mexican Consulate, and local banks.

21. This category includes printed and/or online information materials in the form of brochures/guides/workbooks/fact sheets etc.

22. *www.fms.treas.gov/eft/promotional/helping.html* and *www.nefe.org/amexeconfund/ materials/helpingpeopleinyour.html*.

23. *www.centrelink.gov.au/internet/internet.nsf/ filestores/fis028_0402/$file/ fis028_0402en.pdf*.

24. *www.prosperitycampaign.com* and *www.treas.gov/offices/domestic-finance/financial institution/fin education/*.

25. Nonprofits: HSC, the *John S. and James L. Knight Foundation*, the *Annie E. Casey Foundation*, the North Dade Medical Foundation; government department: the *US Department of Agriculture*.

26. *www.treas.gov/offices/domestic finance/financial institution/fin education/*.

27. *www.fsa.gov.uk/consumer/02_HOW/index.html*.

28. *http://credit.about.com/cs/familyfinances/a/091102.htm*.

29. A pilot programme which ran from July 2001 to March 2002.

30. To be eligible for the FLLIP programme, participants' incomes must be equal to or less than 200 per cent of the poverty level. Moreover, few participants own checking accounts (less than half), and even fewer own savings accounts (two fifths).

31. The curriculum also "takes into account the often limited educational attainment of programme participants".

32. *www.ace.uiuc.edu/cfe/mymoney/*.

33. Often referred to in the literature as the "train the trainer" principle.

34. *www.urbanext.uiuc.edu/chicago/ar2003/fcs3.html*.

35. *www.urbanext.uiuc.edu/chicago/ar2003/fcs3.html*.

36. *www.urbanext.uiuc.edu/chicago/ar2003/fcs3.html*.

37. *www.urbanext.uiuc.edu/chicago/ar2003/fcs3.html*.

References

Anderson, S.G., J. Scott and M. Zhan (2002), Executive Summary of Financial Links for Low-Income People, (FLLIP): Evaluation of Implementation and Initial Training Activity, School of Social Work, University of Illinois at Urbana-Champaign, *www.povertylaw.org/advocacy/community_investment/executive_summary.doc*, accessed December 2004.

Anderson, S.G., J. Scott and M. Zhan (2004a), Executive Summary of Financial Links for Low-Income People, (FLLIP): Final Evaluation Report, School of Social Work, University of Illinois at Urbana-Champaign.

Anderson, S.G., J. Scott and M. Zhan (2004b), Financial Links for Low-Income People, (FLLIP): Final Evaluation Report, School of Social Work, University of Illinois at Urbana-Champaign, *www.povertylaw.org/advocacy/community_investment/documents/ fllip%20fin%20rep%20TOC.pdf*, accessed January 12 2005.

Australian Bankers' Association (ABA) (2000a), Self Service Banking and Older Australians, Project Management Committee, *www.bankers.asn.au/ArticleDocuments/SELFSERVICE.pdf*, accessed December 2004.

Australian Bankers' Association (ABA) (2000b), "Electronic Banking and Financial Services: Providing Convenience and Value", Submission prepared for Inquiry into Fees on Electronic and Telephone Banking, Parliamentary Joint Statutory Committee on Corporations and Securities, *www.bankers.asn.au/ArticleDocuments/20030306%20Fees%20on%20Electronic%20and%20Telephone%20Banking%20sub.doc*, accessed December 2004.

Australian Bankers' Association (ABA) (2004), "New Ways of Banking – overview", ABA Factsheets, Australian Bankers' Association, *www.bankers.asn.au/Default.aspx?ArticleID=620*, accessed January 2005.

Australian Department of Health and Ageing (ADoHA) (1999), "Bishop Kicks Off Self-Service Banking and Older Australians Project at Parramatta Leagues", Press Release, 15 April 1999, *www.health.gov.au/internet/wcms/publishing.nsf/Content/health-mediarel-yr1999-bb-bb99022.htm*, accessed November 2004.

Autumn, S. *et al.* (2003), "Bringing the Unbanked into the Financial Services Market", Consumer Interests Annual, Vol. 40, *http://consumerinterests.org/public/articles/Unbanked_03.pdf*, accessed 16th January 2004.

Braunstein, S. and C. Welch (2002), "Financial Literacy: An Overview of Practice, Research and Policy", Federal Reserve Bulletin, Washington D.C., *www.federalreserve.gov/pubs/bulletin/2002/1102lead.pdf#*, accessed 22 August 2003.

Connolly, C. and K. Hajaj (2001), Financial Services and Social Exclusion, Financial Services Consumer Policy Centre, University Of New South Wales, Chifley Research Centre, *www.chifley.org.au/publications/banking_and_social_exclusion_final_report.pdf*, accessed December 2004.

Dartnall, L. *et al.* (2002), Evaluation of the Community Development Programme in Financial Literacy and Basic Skills, National Foundation for Educational Research (NFER), *www.basic-skills.co.uk#*, accessed 16 July 2003.

Greenspan, A. (2002), "Economic Development and Financial Literacy", Speech given by Chairman Alan Greenspan at the Ninth Annual Economic Development Summit, the Greenlining Institute, Oakland, California, 10 January 2002, *www.federalreserve.gov/boarddocs/speeches/2002/20020110/default.htm* accessed January 2005.

Kempson, E., A. Atkinson and O. Pilley (2004), Policy Level Response To Financial Exclusion In Developed Economies: Lessons For Developing Countries, Personal Finance Research Centre, University of Bristol, Bristol, commissioned by Financial Sector Team, Policy Division, Department for International Development, UK, *www.microfinancegateway.org/files/21955_dfid_report.pdf* accessed October 2004.

Malkin, J. (2003), "Financial Education in Native Communities: A Briefing Paper", paper presented at the Native American Financial Literacy Coalition's Financial Education in Native Communities national policy development forum, 28-29 May 2003, Denver, Colorado, *www.cfed.org/publications/Financial Education in Native Communities.pdf*, accessed 26 August 2003.

Partee, G. " (2001),Young Adults And Welfare-To-Work: Lessons For The United States From The UK And Australia", Brief from an American Youth Policy Forum, 5 November 2001, Capitol Hill, Washington D.C., *www.aypf.org/forumbriefs/2001/fb110501.htm* accessed November 2004.

Robles, B. (2004), "Is Your Credit Union Hispanic Market Ready?", presentation prepared for Credit Union National Association's (CUNA) Ninth Annual Discovery Conference 2004, Experience the Power, San Diego, 9-12 June, *www.utexas.edu/lbj/faculty/robles/projects/ppt/CUNA_June10.ppt*, accessed January 2005.

Social and Enterprise Development Innovations (SEDI) (2004), "Financial Capability and Poverty", Discussion Paper, Policy Research Initiative, Ottawa, Canada, *http://policyresearch.gc.ca/doclib/Poverty_SEDI_final_E.pdf*, accessed June 2005.

Stegman, M.A. (1998), "Electronic Benefit's Potential to Help the Poor", Policy Brief, No. 32, The Brookings Institution, Washington D.C., *www.brookings.org/printme.wbs?page=/comm/policybriefs/pb32.htm*, accessed December 2004.

US Federal Reserve Bank of Chicago (USFRB Chicago) (2001), "Fostering Mainstream Financial Access: *www.chicagofed.org/unbanked*", Chicago Fed Newsletter, No. 162, *www.chicagofed.org/publications/fedletter/2001/cflfeb2001_162.pdf*, accessed 23 January 2004.

US Federal Reserve Bank of Dallas (USFRB Dallas) (2002), "Banking on Safety: Banks Accept Alternative KID to Fight Crime and Reach New Markets", E-Perspectives Online, Vol. 2, Issue 1, *www.dallasfed.org/ca/epersp/2002/1_2.html*, accessed November 2004.

Williams, J.M. (2002), Statement prepared for Hearing on Bringing More Unbanked Americans into the Financial Mainstream, Committee on Banking, Housing, and Urban Affairs, The United States Senate One Hundred Seventh Congress, Second Session, 2 May 2002, Washington, *http://banking.senate.gov/_files/107946.pdf*, accessed January 2005.

Internet References

All My Money Web site on the Web site of the University of Illinois at Urbana-Champaign: [*www.ace.uiuc.edu/cfe/mymoney/*] (accessed November 2004).

All My Money Web site on the Web site of the University of Illinois Extension, Chicago unit: [*www.urbanext.uiuc.edu/chicago/ar2003/fcs3.html*] (accessed November 2004).

Connecticut Individual Development Account Initiative: [*www.ctdol.state.ct.us/ida/dir/finedu.html*] (accessed November 2004).

Department of Family and Community Services, Australian Government: [*www.facs.gov.au*] (accessed January 2005).

Greater Miami Prosperity Campaign: [*www.prosperitycampaign.com*] (accessed December 2004).

Hawaiian Community Assets: [*www.ruralisc.org/hca.htm*] (accessed December 2004).

How to Save on Fees and Charges, Centrelink (Australia) factsheet: [*www.centrelink.gov.au/internet/internet.nsf/filestores/fis028_0402/$file/fis028_0402en.pdf*] (accessed November 2004).

IDA Network: [*www.idanetwork.org*] (accessed November 2004).

Information on Helping People in Your Community Understand Basic Financial Services on the Web site of the Financial Management Service of the United States Treasury: [*www.fms.treas.gov/eft/promotional/helping.html*] (accessed November 2004).

Information on Helping People in Your Community Understand Basic Financial Services on the Web site of the National Endowment for Financial Education, United States: [*www.nefe.org/amexeconfund/materials/helpingpeopleinyour.html*] (accessed November 2004).

Migration Watch United Kingdom: [*www.migrationwatchuk.org*] (accessed April 2005).

National Endowment for Financial Education : [*www.nefe.org*] (accessed December 2004).

Office of Financial Education, United States Treasury: [*www.treas.gov*] (accessed December 2004).

ANNEX E

Recommendation on Principles and Good Practices for Financial Education and Awareness

RECOMMENDATION OF THE COUNCIL JULY 2005

THE COUNCIL,

Having regard to Article 5b) of the Convention on the Organisation for Economic Co-operation and Development of 14th December 1960;

Considering that, as financial education has always been important for consumers in helping them budget and manage their income, save and invest efficiently, and avoid becoming victims of fraud;

Considering that as financial markets become increasingly sophisticated and households assume more of the responsibility and risk for financial decisions, especially in the field of retirement savings, financially educated individuals are necessary to ensure sufficient levels of investor and consumer protection as well as the smooth functioning, not only of financial markets, but also of the economy;

Considering that surveys of financial literacy conducted in recent years in OECD countries show that consumers have low levels of financial literacy and lack awareness of the need to be financially educated;

Considering that governments and relevant public and private institutions (at national and sub-national level and including regulatory and supervisory bodies) in OECD and non-OECD countries may benefit from international guidance on principles and good practices for financial education and awareness;

Considering that their implementation will have to take into consideration various economic, social, demographic and cultural factors and, thus, will vary from country to country and that there are also numerous methods to develop successfully financial education for a particular audience;

Considering also that the implementation of the good practices related to financial institutions needs to take into consideration the diversity of financial institutions, that these guidelines do not prevent relevant commercial activities and that national associations of financial institutions are expected to be the main players for this sub-set of good practices;

On the proposal of the Committee of Financial Markets:

RECOMMENDS that member countries promote financial education and awareness and in this respect that governments and relevant public and private institutions take due account of and implement the principles and good practices for financial education and awareness which are set out in the annex to this Recommendation and form an integral part thereof.

INVITES member countries to disseminate these principles and good practices among public and private (profit and not-for-profit) sector institutions that are involved in financial education and awareness.

INVITES Non-member economies to take due account of this Recommendation and to disseminate these principles and good practices among public and private (profit and not-for-profit) sector institutions that are involved in financial education and awareness.

INVITES member countries, through their work in the Committee on Financial Markets, the Insurance Committee and its Working Party on Private Pensions, to identify further good practices respectively in financial, insurance and pension education field.

INSTRUCTS the Committee on Financial Markets to exchange information on progress and experiences with respect to the implementation of this Recommendation, review that information and report to the Council within three years of its adoption, or sooner, and, as appropriate, thereafter.

PRINCIPLES AND GOOD PRACTICES
FOR FINANCIAL EDUCATION AND AWARENESS

I. Principles

1. Financial education can be defined as "the process by which financial consumers/investors improve their understanding of financial products, concepts and risks and, through information, instruction and/or objective advice, develop the skills and confidence to become more aware of financial risks and opportunities, to make informed choices, to know where to go for help, and to take other effective actions to improve their financial well-being". Financial education thus goes beyond the provision of financial information and advice, which should be regulated, as is already often the case, in particular for the protection of financial clients (*i.e.* consumers in contractual relationships).

2. This financial capacity building, based on proper financial information and instruction, should be promoted. Financial education should be provided in a fair and unbiased manner. Programmes should be co-ordinated and developed with efficiency.

3. Financial education programmes should focus on high priority issues, which, depending on national circumstances, may include important aspects of financial life planning such as basic savings, private debt management or insurance as well as pre-requisites for financial awareness such as elementary financial mathematics and economics. The awareness of future retirees about the need to assess the financial adequacy of their current public or private pensions schemes and to take appropriate action when needed should be encouraged.

4. Financial education should be taken into account in the regulatory and administrative framework and considered as a tool to promote economic growth, confidence and stability, together with regulation of financial institutions and consumer protection (including the regulation of financial information and advice). The promotion of financial education should not be substituted for financial regulation, which is essential to protect consumers (for instance against fraud) and which financial education is expected to complement.

5. Appropriate measures should be taken when financial capacity is essential but deficiencies are observed. Other policy tools to consider are consumer protection and financial institution regulation. Without limiting the freedom to contract, default mechanisms, which take into consideration inadequate financial education or passive/inert behaviour, should be considered.

6. The role of financial institutions in financial education should be promoted and become part of their good governance with respect to their financial clients. Financial institutions' accountability and responsibility should be encouraged not only in providing information and advice on financial issues, but also in promoting financial awareness clients, especially for long-term commitments and commitments which represent a substantial proportion of current and future income.

7. Financial education programmes should be designed to meet the needs and the financial literacy level of their target audience, as well as reflect how their target audience prefers to receive financial information. Financial education should be regarded as a life-time, on-going and continuous process, in particular in order to take account of the increased complexity of markets, varying needs at different life stages, and increasingly complex information.

II. Good practices

A. Public action for financial education

8. National campaigns should be encouraged to raise awareness of the population about the need to improve their understanding of financial risks and ways to protect against financial risks through adequate savings, insurance and financial education.

9. Financial education should start at school. People should be educated about financial matters as early as possible in their lives.

10. Consideration should be given to making financial education a part of state welfare assistance programmes.

11. Appropriate specialised structures (possibly embedded within existing authorities) in charge of promoting and coordinating financial education should be encouraged at the national level and regional and local public and private initiatives as close to the population as possible should also be promoted.

12. Specific Web sites should be promoted to provide relevant, user-friendly financial information to the public. Free information services should be developed. Warning systems by consumer, professional or other organisation on high-risk issues that may be detrimental to the interests of the financial consumers (including cases of fraud) should be promoted.

13. International co-operation on financial education should be promoted, including the use of the OECD as an international forum to exchange information on recent national experiences in financial education.

B. Role of financial institutions in financial education

14. Requirements to specify the types of information (including where to find information and the provision of general comparative and objective information on the risks and returns of different kinds of products) that financial institutions need to provide to clients on financial products and services, should be encouraged.

15. Financial institutions should be encouraged to clearly distinguish between financial education and financial information and "commercial" financial advice. Any financial advice for business purposes should be transparent and disclose clearly any commercial nature where it is also being promoted as a financial education initiative. For those financial services that entail long-term commitment or have potentially significant financial consequences, financial institutions should be encouraged to check that the information provided to their clients is read and understood.

16. Financial institutions should be encouraged to provide information at several different levels in order to best meet the needs of consumers. Small print, abstruse documentation should be discouraged.

17. Financial education provided by financial institutions should be regularly assessed to ensure it meets consumer needs. This may be achieved through partnerships with independent, not for profit financial advisory bodies that may have better connection with consumers, particularly those facing disadvantage in their participation in financial markets.

18. Financial institutions should be encouraged to train their staff on financial education and develop codes of conduct for the provision of general advice about investment and borrowing, not linked to the supply of a specific product.

C. Financial education for retirement savings

19. For individuals in private personal pension plans, the provision by financial institutions of the appropriate financial information and education required for the management of their future retirement savings and income should be promoted.

20. Concerning occupational schemes, (for which the related information and education should be provided in a consistent way across the schemes) financial education and awareness of employees and related policy tools should be further promoted, both for defined contributions and defined benefits schemes.

D. *Financial education programmes*

21. Financial education programmes that help financial consumers find the facts and understand the pros and cons as well as the risks of different types of financial products and services should be promoted. Further research on behavioural economics should be promoted.

22. The development of methodologies to assess existing financial education programmes should be promoted. Official recognition of financial education programmes which fulfil relevant criteria should be considered.

23. Financial education programmes that develop guidelines on study content and accomplishment level for each financial education programme and for each population subgroup should be promoted.

24. In order to achieve a wider coverage and exposure, the use of all available media for the dissemination of education messages should be promoted.

25. In order to take into account the diverse backgrounds of investors/consumers, financial education that creates different programmes for specific sub-groups of investors/consumers (*i.e.* young people, the less educated, disadvantaged groups) should be promoted. Financial education should be related to the individual circumstance, through financial education seminars and personalised financial counselling programmes.

26. For those programmes which favour use of classrooms, proper education and competence of the educators should be promoted. In this respect, the development of programmes to "train the trainers" and the provision of specific information material and tools for these trainers should be encouraged.

OECD PUBLICATIONS, 2, rue André-Pascal, 75775 PARIS CEDEX 16
PRINTED IN FRANCE
(21 2005 10 1 P) ISBN 92-64-01256-7 – No. 54259 2005